Broken Covenant

BROKEN COVENANT

A Divorce Memoir

Rebecca Carroll

FITHIAN PRESS, SANTA BARBARA, CALIFORNIA, 2000

Published by Fithian Press
A division of Daniel and Daniel, Publishers, Inc.
Post Office Box 1525
Santa Barbara, CA 93102
www.danielpublishing.com

LIBRARY OF CONGRESS CATALOGING-IN-PUBLICATION DATA
Carroll, Rebecca F., (date)
    Broken covenant : a divorce memoir / by Rebecca F. Carroll.
    p. cm.
    ISBN 1-56474-327-6 (pbk.)
    1. Carroll, Rebecca F. (date) 2. Divorced women—Biography. 3. Divorce—
Religious aspects—Christianity. I. Title.
    HQ814.C345 2000
    305.48'9653'092—dc21   00-008172

To Samantha von der Heydt

and

Mike Serio

Contents

Broken Covenant

Introduction

It was a painful experience going through separation and divorce, especially since my heritage included an overexposure to a Protestant, evangelical Christian doctrine. But I instinctively turned to religion for comfort and hope during my divorce and recovery. Although prior to my divorce I had come to reject my former belief system, in the confusion and pain of divorce, I cried to God for strength.

My story began in the Bible belt, where my forefathers took the Bible literally, where mothers taught daughters to save their virginity for their future husbands, where the church taught its sons to drive lustful thoughts of women from their minds. These beliefs, along with others from the church doctrine in which I was raised, had a profoundly negative effect on my sex life, marriage, recovery from divorce and my self-knowledge. In comparing my divorce with others' from my former religion, I found variations on the same themes; similar experiences to mine had also happened to others. I then realized the severity of the circumstances. Overexposure to a strict, religious lifestyle had adversely affected the self-awareness of countless numbers of couples—as innocent and naive as my former husband and I, and equally as baffled about how to correct their situation.

My book was written for this audience. However, since generalizations can be made about the process of divorce and recovery my journal will also be relevant to those men and women interested in personal growth through examining the emotional aspects of divorce.

I began my divorce journal eleven months after my husband and I separated. Every day during my eighty-minute train ride to work, I wrote about my separation/divorce experiences, dreams, the pain I faced and whatever was foremost in my mind during that troubled year. My writing continued for fourteen months. Five years later, after having laid it aside, I began to add to and edit my journal. This experience was extremely rewarding, for through this work I came to understand how the religious background in which my former husband and I were raised played a role in the dynamics of our marriage, our physical relationship and our divorce.

It is my hope that by sharing the emotions, pain, and the lessons learned from my divorce experience, others may benefit. May they be encouraged with the knowledge that they are not alone and that others have also walked along their path.

Note: All names except mine have been changed to preserve confidentiality.

1. Settlement

Eleven Months of Separation

I was living alone in a cottage I had rented in Groton, Massachusetts, after leaving my husband of fifteen years.

I heard a knock at my door; my heart stood still. Jonathan had filed for divorce and he came today at my request to take care of settlement details because I thought it would be easier and more efficient than relaying messages through our lawyers. It was important to me that Jonathan felt good about the fairness of our settlement, so I suggested we meet at my cottage to discuss the details together.

As I opened my front door, Jonathan walked toward his car, lifted the rear door, and nervously called to me, "Grab your coat and help me carry in these things." Was that quick command indicative that he was uncomfortable seeing me again?

My husband reminded me of a young boy bringing presents to his mother. He eagerly sought my approval—acknowledgment that yes, he had chosen an item from my past that was special. If only he knew he bore vessels of pain.

We carried into my bedroom the boxes that contained mementos of my former life, reminders of a time that had been better. How many memories were associated with each item! My life had been transplanted into my new surroundings and now, likewise, these boxes arrived with things from my past.

There was the desk lamp we used on our night stand. The lamp was extremely top-heavy, because it had a large metal shade. I had lost count of the times it had toppled off the stand next to our bed and fallen to the floor. The glass globe had been broken and re-glued, evidence of its poor design. The lamp evoked memories of a time when Jonathan and I slept in the same bed and turned off the light every night before going to sleep.

Jonathan handed me some slides; I held them to the window. The slides were of my bike trip to Cape Cod with two girlfriends. One showed me looking across the lake near our camp site as though I was trying to see the future. Could I have seen what was going to happen to us?

I wanted Jonathan to like my cottage, to approve of the way I had furnished and decorated it. I showed him with pride my new Belgian carpets and my stereo speakers. Since I wanted him to appreciate my resourcefulness, I also showed him the bathroom curtains I made from two towels. Whether he acted impressed or actually was, I don't know, but he afforded me the tiny bits of approval I seemed to need.

We walked into the kitchen. "See this table I assembled and stained myself?" I asked proudly. "It was unfinished, and I got it very cheaply." I wanted him to know I wasn't being extravagant and that I was using my money wisely. I partially removed the table cloth to show Jonathan the wood, on which I had brushed eight coats of tung oil.

"Good job, Becky," Jonathan said. Maybe if I showed him enough good things he would be impressed and he would start to love me again. Maybe if he saw that I was a good, productive person on my own, he would forgive me and take me back.

"Well, let's take care of business," Jonathan said. I was shocked, although I expected his words; he hadn't changed his mind. He still wanted a divorce. I was hoping we could put the business part off indefinitely and forget about the divorce forever. But Jonathan wanted to discuss the settlement now.

My lawyer had advised me to sue for alimony, but I was not interested. However, when he told me that accumulated retirement funds were usually divided, I asked for a settlement of half— $7,000. Since I had left Jonathan with our only car, the settlement would pay for the car I had to buy.

I began, "I'd rather have the money now to help with my start-up expenses instead of later for retirement when I'm already established." I felt I had to justify my request.

Jonathan quietly said, "I've given a lot of thought to this, and I'm prepared to leave you a check today. I don't think you should pay all the taxes on this. We'll divide the taxes, and I'll leave you a check now."

He looked at me, then asked, "Did I say something wrong?"

Tears were streaming down my face. The tears were not only in appreciation of the money, but because it hurt. "I'm sorry, Jonathan. I didn't want to make this more painful by crying."

"It's okay," he said. "Would this arrangement be helpful to you?"

"Be helpful? It's very generous. Of course it would be helpful, but let me think about this." The money didn't seem important. I wanted him.

"I've given a lot of thought to this, and if we can be flexible, I will pay you monthly until the debt is paid off." Again he said, "I am prepared to leave you a check today."

Why did we have to do this? I would take the check but save it. If we reconciled it could be returned to Jonathan. I wanted my husband—not a check.

"Did I say something wrong?" he asked again.

I could not respond.

"You must go to your rehearsal," Jonathan said. "Isn't it past time for you to leave?" I had told Jonathan in our last phone conversation that I was playing chamber music today.

"I was going to cancel because, after all, how often do I see you? My music friends knew you were coming today and they told me to come when I could."

"It's probably wise that you didn't cancel," Jonathan said.

Oh, but why didn't he want to stay just a little longer? My dream was that he would miss me so much he would want to spend the whole day with me—and then another and then forget the divorce.

"But..." I wanted to delay his departure. "But did you understand why I had to leave you? I had to heal myself. Of course, I realize I'm asking a lot—for the person I've hurt to forgive me and then be understanding."

There was a pause.

"But, Jonathan," I asked desperately, "are we doing the right thing?" I was still asking his opinion, even in divorce.

"Yes. I believe we are," Jonathan answered. "I believe I can't make you happy, and that our relationship has been lost."

"But you can't decide for me. Only I can decide what makes me happy. Your argument is not scientific—not valid." I was feebly trying to appeal to his logical mind.

"Well, there are other things too." He hesitated then added, "I wrote you about Sharon. She's become a very supportive friend."

Why was he talking about his girlfriend, Sharon? Where was his heart? Couldn't he feel what I felt—that there was still love between us? The feeling of love overwhelmed me; it was there with us in my little kitchen. I could feel it as plainly as one feels the sunshine's warmth, but Jonathan was indifferent, untouched, left out.

As he left my cottage that day, tears blurred my vision and washed my kitchen white with pain. I felt an overwhelming love for this man who had spent fifteen years with me and who was still legally my husband. Although we had not been together for one year, my love for him had grown and had bridged our separation.

"Couldn't we use what we learned during this year to make our marriage work now? Oh, Jonathan, couldn't we?" There was no answer. Jonathan was gone. All I could do was think about him— how wonderful he was—and then ask myself how I had allowed our marriage to come to this. "Oh, God, please give him back to me. I'll be good, I promise."

For a few hours that Saturday, it almost seemed as though time had been reversed and we were sharing the same apartment, the same bank account, the same bed. But it was the present, and things were not the same. Now all was different. We were moving toward divorce, toward ending our eighteen-year association with one another, and going on with our lives, separately.

I was not attending church regularly, as I had with my husband, but I was aware of God's presence in my life—not in a personal way, but generally, especially through the difficult stages of my divorce. The fact that I was able to find my charming cottage to rent seemed designed by God.

The cottage was exactly to my liking. It was very private, on a farm in the country, and, most importantly, it was aesthetically pleasing. The forest bordered my living room windows; I did not need curtains. This was the perfect place for an artist—private and surrounded by beauty.

I love nature, and my cottage was adjacent to paths in the woods that led to a beautiful lake. Sometimes when I went to the lake, I said a prayer for Jonathan and me. Although I was uncertain whether I should pray for reconciliation, I simply prayed that God would be with Jonathan and take care of him.

I called my religious college friend, Barbara Hachett, who was living in Holland. The call was to follow-up on a letter I had written to her several months earlier. Following is our phone conversation:

"Did you receive my letter?" I asked.

"Yes, I did," Barbara replied, "and of course I've been in contact with Jonathan, too. You know that I'm going to remain friends with both of you."

"So you've been in contact with Jonathan?" I asked.

"Yes. In fact, he wrote to ask if he and his mother could stay with me during their trip to Europe. Of course, I said it was okay."

I didn't want to discuss Jonathan's plan to visit Barbara, so I asked, "When are you coming back to America?"

"Not for three years at least. Financially, we can't afford it."

"I wish you were close by," I said. Then I paused. "I'm calling to ask for your prayers. I want to have a 'heavy-duty' Christian to pray for me and Jonathan."

"So you are on speaking terms with God now?" Barbara questioned.

"Yes, I am. You see, I think Jonathan's heart is softening."

"Jonathan's heart is softening! Jonathan's heart has always been soft!" Barbara said. "Maybe it's your heart that is softening!"

"Maybe. Jonathan came over a few days ago to discuss our divorce settlement, and during that time I felt that he cared for me still. I mean, he wasn't overly emotional and he didn't give me any indication of hope for reconciliation, but I could almost close my eyes and imagine that we were still living together as husband and wife. He brought me some things from his apartment that he thought I'd like, and he seemed happy to see me. You see, I thought if I could have several 'heavy-duty' Christians praying for me and Jonathan, maybe God would change Jonathan's mind."

"So you're on speaking terms with God now?" Barbara repeated. "That makes a difference. Now there is something to work with! I think the straw that broke the camel's back, so to speak, was your involvement with another man last summer. I think until that point Jonathan would have taken you back. I'm being very blunt now, but are you repentant for what you've done?" She continued before I had a chance to answer. "I remember last year, you said you weren't sorry, and in fact you were glad you had committed adultery. Are you now sorry?"

"Oh, yes! Yes! Every day I regret with all my heart the sins I've committed," I answered.

"Do you think you can now be happy with Jonathan?"

"Oh, yes. I know I can be happy with him, because now I am happy on my own, so I can be happy with him," I answered. "Aside from missing Jonathan, I'm rather content with my new life. I've got a great place in the country, a good job, friends, and musical activities."

"Yes, your cottage as you described it in your letter sounds lovely," Barbara said.

"I don't know at this point what is best," I said. "I just want what is best for me and Jonathan. If it's best that we don't reconcile, then I want that. But it doesn't seem like it would be God's will for us to become divorced. Do you have any suggestions?"

"Are you attending church now?" Barbara asked.

"On occasion. I go to an Anglican church in Boston," I said. "The music is beautiful."

"I suggest that you become involved in a Bible study! Are you presently involved in one?"

"No."

"You should be in a Bible study! I know when I could no longer go on, my involvement in a Bible study carried me through."

"I will keep that in mind," I said.

"And obey God's laws! They are not to be broken!"

"Yes, I will," I answered. "I am being very good now."

"I can't promise any outcome," Barbara said, "or say what is best, either. But be assured that prayers are continuing on your and Jonathan's behalf."

"I guess I have nothing to lose," I said.

In a digging tone of voice, Barbara added, "Yes, you have nothing to lose at this point."

After that conversation, and after being scolded by my righteous friend, I felt the little glimmer of hope for Jonathan and me extinguish. What right had I to think that Jonathan would come back to me? I hadn't the right to ask him to come back. I was, after all, the sinner, and now I had to pay.

I kept reaching out to Jonathan with my whole being, even in my sleep. In my dreams I asked him if I could come back, but he would shake his head no. Perhaps because he would not take me back in reality, I thought he would in my dreams. These dreams recurred many times.

One night I was hurt doubly because I dreamed of Jonathan twice. I saw him dressed in a red T-shirt with khaki pants. He had a pillowcase full of clothes flung over his shoulder like a hobo. I knew he was leaving me. Again I asked him if we could reconcile, but the answer was no. Then I awoke all alone, in my dark cottage, in the night.

"Oh, what have I done? Oh, God, why did I leave him?" No one heard the cries from my heart that rang deep into the night, and I felt no one cared. I cried out to God again. "Can't you change his mind, God? Can't you perform a miracle? Can't you bring him back?"

The hot tears flowed down the side of my face, down my temples, and into my hair. Was God paying me back for my sins? Did I suffer so I could be purified? Although I had tried to succeed in my marriage, I was not judged by my efforts but by my results; in my marriage I had failed. I closed my eyes again to shut out the night and the pain.

Again my sleep was troubled. The devil of the night had come again to torment me. The images I saw didn't appear real. It was as though my husband's picture had been pasted to a wand that was being drawn back and forth in front of my eyes. I knew it was not Jonathan who was trying to terrorize me, but an evil force that knew my vulnerabilities and was using Jonathan's image against the black backdrop of the night to make me cry out in terror. I was helpless, with no ability to control the speed of the wand or its closeness to me. The image kept dancing before me as the goblins in Berlioz's *Symphonie fantastique*, until I physically cried out and woke myself from the nightmare.

I remember that when I had nightmares in the past, my husband would gently touch my arm and awaken me, then he would pull me close into his arms and next to his warm body. Awakening from nightmares alone in my bed, without anyone to comfort me, sharply contrasted the present with my former life. How much more painful it was to be alone.

"Fear thou not, for thou art with me. Be not dismayed, for I am thy God. I will strengthen thee, I will help thee, I will uphold thee with my righteous right hand." (Isaiah 41:10) During my separation, I kept repeating the scripture over and over so that the truth would sink into my being. I needed something solid to hold on to—something to keep me from falling, for it felt as though the floor was unstable, that it was rocking wildly back and forth,

making me frenzied. "Fear thou not." My vision was blurry; my
head felt ponderous. It was as though time had stopped and the
focus of the universe was pain and tribulation. How could I endure
it? "...for thou art with me. Be not dismayed, for I am thy God."
It had been a year since we last lived together, so I couldn't understand how there could still be so much pain. I was sobbing deeply
as I cried out to God, "Please give me back my husband! Oh,
God—I still love him so! Please give him back to me!"

I flung myself onto the couch and mashed my face into the pillows. There was no one to answer, no one to care, no one to comfort me. My cottage, my place of refuge, could not hug me, stroke
my head, or kiss away my tears. My cries bounced off the windows
and walls and returned to me unheard, except perhaps by God.

Love needs a recipient; it is a tragedy when there is love and no
partner. Perfect love is the oneness of heart with its object, but
since the real world is not perfect, neither is love. One can carry
love alone, but without the proper response from its object, it will
weaken and die. Imperfect love is when the two do not make a full
connection, but the sparks generated from trying keep them together. Intimate love, close to perfection, is the total union of body,
soul and spirit. It forms between two lovers an electric, lightning-
like chain through which communication flows, resulting in perfect unity and understanding. It's through this keen sensitivity that
I feel my longings can be satisfied.

I now felt alone in carrying my love. I tried to make a connection with Jonathan, but there were only disconnected sparks. We
did not understand each other, and now he was gone. The love I
felt was only me reaching out. It was only my half; it would not be
whole, because there was no recipient. How very sad that such a
wealth of love could not be received through the proper channel.

2. The Beginning

Nineteen Years Prior

Jonathan and I met at a small, church-supported Christian college near Boston during my freshman year. I was from Baltimore, Maryland, majoring in music education; he was from Erie, Pennsylvania, majoring in science. My friend Barbara Hachett, who had a crush on him, introduced us. In an unexpected turn of events, Jonathan became my boyfriend instead of hers.

At the beginning of our dating experience, Jonathan and I clearly had problems understanding one another. Daily, it seemed, his behavior toward me caused confusion and bewilderment. On one occasion he called to say he had missed seeing me in church. He suggested that perhaps I was avoiding him because he "bugged" me. Laughingly I replied, "Sure, Jonathan, you bug me a lot!" He responded, "Okay, I'll leave you alone then," and he hung up the phone. I didn't know what to think! His behavior left me hurt and confused. Later that evening I called him and asked that we meet to discuss what had happened. During our meeting he told me the whole thing had been a joke. Although I had failed to see the humor, I believed that he had been attempting to tease me.

I tolerated Jonathan's unusual behavior because I believed he had not wanted to hurt me and that he was very inexperienced at dating. Also, I rationalized that since he had no sisters, he didn't know how to relate to women. I patiently tried to help him sort out his unusual behavior in our relationship, and in time the number of these incidents decreased.

However, Jonathan was not the only one who was confused. Two or three times within five months of dating I became very entangled in trying to discover God's will regarding me and Jonathan through prayer and listening for God's direction. At one point, I informed Jonathan that God had revealed to me that our relationship should end. We went through the formalities of breaking up, then resumed our relationship as though we were still together, for I hadn't really wanted to stop seeing him. Then guilt consumed me because I thought I was disobeying God. Jonathan, being more logical, finally convinced me I wasn't disobeying God and that I was wrong in my interpretation of God's will.

Our personalities were so opposite that they complemented each other. I helped him learn how to behave more appropriately in a relationship, and he helped me learn to use my head more instead of my emotions. We were half-people alone—together we made a whole. Several months later our relationship stabilized, and we fell in love. Our partnership had begun of mutual trust and respect. It would last over seventeen years.

Our courtship was not based on a physical relationship. Because our religious beliefs forbade premarital sex, we had strict rules regarding what we could and could not do. Kissing was allowed; petting was not. Although our two-and-a-half-year dating period included many kissing sessions, we agreed not to progress further until marriage. Our love was expressed in other ways: through presents, love notes, kind words and deeds.

Our dating experience frequently included activities that were centered around the church, since we wanted our relationship to be God-centered. We attended church services, prayed, and had our devotions together. During the school year we ate our meals together in the college dining hall, studied, and walked on the beach. During our summer vacations we visited one another and picked blueberries, swam, canoed, and hiked. (Only three times did we see a movie together, for it was prohibited by our church manual, as was drinking alcoholic beverages and dancing.)

In many ways I idolized Jonathan. I was grateful that he had brought an emotional stability into my life; I considered him my hero. I admired his intelligence, goodness, honesty, and godliness. Because I believed him to be so much better than me, if something negative happened in our relationship I dismissed it or thought I was at fault. To me, Jonathan was almost above wrongdoing.

Although there were times during our dating when I wished Jonathan would show me more affection, I believed my attitude, not his behavior, needed changing. At public events where school friends attended, I felt that he treated me as one of the guys because he frequently left me alone. Although his behavior toward me sometimes made me feel taken for granted, instead of mentioning this to him I decided I was being immature. I rationalized that since he wasn't insecure like me, he wasn't affectionate because he didn't need someone constantly stroking him to reaffirm his esteem. Because I loved Jonathan and looked up to him, I accepted his approach to our relationship and disregarded what I wanted.

During our two years of dating, we learned to depend upon one another for support and love. As a result, our relationship grew stronger. As it matured, we decided we would marry after we both graduated from college. However, at the end of my sophomore year I left college because I was afraid of accumulating a large debt, since I was paying my own way. While living with my parents I stayed on at my summer job as a receptionist in Baltimore so that I could save the cost of tuition for my last two years.

As Jonathan continued his education in Boston, the separation became too difficult for us. Our urgent desire to be together began to outweigh everything else, so I decided that we should marry within the year. By Thanksgiving we were engaged, and less than four months later we were married, only two weeks after Jonathan finished classes. I was twenty-one and he was twenty-two when I moved from Baltimore to Boston and we began our new life together as husband and wife.

My plans to continue school were postponed, for my savings went toward our church wedding. Within several weeks of becoming settled in our apartment, I found full-time work as a claims examiner at Blue Cross Blue Shield. Jonathan continued taking extra courses part time while working part time with the greenhouse crew at our Christian college.

Although I tried not to dwell upon it, our honeymoon was extremely disappointing to me. Something was wrong with our sex life, but I wasn't sure how much was due to our inexperience, since we both were virgins. In the first month of our marriage I bought books about sex for both of us—one for Jonathan and one for me. Although I eagerly read mine, Jonathan never read his. He had very little interest in me sexually and approached me only twice the first month of our marriage. When I asked him why this was so, he replied that he knew I had been sick and he had not wanted to bother me. Although I accepted his explanation because I had been ill with the flu, my recovery made no difference.

Intercourse before marriage was seen by our church as fornication, so I believe it was difficult for Jonathan to participate in behavior after marriage that was seen as sinful before. The switch to a mode that allowed intercourse was too difficult for him to handle all at once. Instead of being excited about discovering the new unexplored area of sex, he instead preferred to remain in his well-established comfort zones, where he was not required to forge ahead and learn through trial and error. So he avoided sex and made light of it by laughing at me when I tried to interest him sexually. This made me feel very unwanted. The pain of being physically rejected as a new bride stayed with me for many years.

Salty tears rolled down my face as I cried at night. Couldn't he hear them loudly drop onto my pillow dampened with pain? Why didn't he caress my breasts then cover them with kisses? Couldn't he taste the bitterness of his unfulfilled lover's desire hovering in the darkness? Why didn't the fragrance of my virginity entice him? Why didn't he softly touch my curves and then pull me close—so close that his body could become part of mine? We were in the same bed yet I felt more lonely than if he were a thousand miles away. The void only echoed my loneliness, for I knew my husband would never be my lover.

•

Even after several months of marriage our sex life had not improved. The following quotes from my diary indicated my concern:

> Sometimes I feel lonely and slightly depressed when Jonathan takes no notice of me. If I'd take all my clothes off in front of him, he'd keep reading [first month of marriage]; I put on my nightgown and tried to look nice and sexy for Jonathan but he didn't seem to notice. I kissed him and sat on his lap, but no response... [second month of marriage]; Jonathan makes me so mad sometimes. When I try and be sexy, he makes fun of me. Why doesn't he think sex is exciting? He watches TV more than me. What's wrong?

Since I had never had a physical relationship before that had included intercourse, I did not know for certain if our situation was typical. However, when girlfriends who had just become married told me of their cystitis or honeymoon's disease, I began to suspect that my situation was unique and abnormal.

I saw a couple on the subway who almost moved me to tears. They were sitting close together—the fellow with his arm around his girlfriend. As if she was too far away, he gently pulled her closer. This display of affection made me yearn for a closeness with my husband which I did not have. As he pulled her close I longed for Jonathan to pull me close. As she snuggled close to her true love, so I wanted to snuggle close to Jonathan. I wished that Jonathan loved me more so that we could have the same kind of love and closeness I saw.

At the beginning of our marriage, in spite of our sexual difficulties, I was very happy because marriage was a new and exciting experience and I loved Jonathan very much. I had never lived on my own, so it was an adventure having an apartment and household effects for the first time. I enjoyed cooking, being domestic and trying to please my husband. Our support system was already in place because our apartment was near the college we had attended and most of our friends were still in the area. Frequently we had company for dinner and spent time with other Christian couples.

I felt the greatest achievement of my life was my marriage to Jonathan. It was wonderful waking up in the morning and finding myself next to him. I loved my husband and I knew he loved me too. For this I was thankful.

Jonathan was gentle and kind. He brought me orange juice when I was sick and he made me feel appreciated when he complimented my cooking. He lifted my spirits by making me laugh. I felt happy and blessed for I knew the Lord was watching over us; He was providing all our needs. I knew our life together as husband and wife would be wonderful. We were very happy and I thanked God for our marriage.

He teased me relentlessly, like a schoolboy, and he made me laugh. I knew he cared, even though his ways of showing it were non-affectionate and awkward. But it did not matter; he loved me, and I knew it. His trust and devotion were unwavering. He would never be romantic or passionate, but I could be content with that, I thought. I was originally attracted to him for his individuality, and I still loved him for this reason and others. Let me now be happy with only the knowledge of his love, and let me require no more, I prayed.

Jonathan was accepted into a master's program in biology at Edinboro State College, so we prepared to move from Boston to Erie, Pennsylvania. It had been my idea for me to stay behind in Boston to work for two additional weeks while Jonathan moved our belongings to Erie. I knew the money from two more pay-checks would come in handy during our time of transition, but I didn't know how lonely it would be without him. My first night of sleeping alone since marriage, I could not rest. I missed Jonathan and wanted my bedmate next to me.

After several weeks I rejoined Jonathan in Erie at his parents' house. Until I could find a job that would allow us to afford our own apartment, we would be staying with the Shaws. Every day while he was in school, I persistently looked for work. I went to employment services, applied at offices, factories, hospitals, and answered newspaper ads. Every day my search was fruitless; my discouragement increased. In addition, I felt pressure to adhere to my in-laws' expectations. I tried my best to please them by cleaning their house and volunteering to cook for them. I became active in their local church, singing solos, playing piano, and teaching Sunday school. This, of course, pleased them immensely.

Living with Jonathan's family increased the common bonds between us, for I developed relationships with my in-laws: Jonathan's brothers and their wives, and his parents (most of the Shaw family lived near Erie). There were many family activities in which we participated, such as picnics on Lake Erie, swimming, Sunday dinners after church, and playing board games after dinner. But all the Shaw activities were secondary to attending church and showing devotion to God.

How could a bridegroom deposit his bride of sixteen months, into the home of his parents, leaving her daily while he attended school? Didn't he have an instinctive male ego, that urged him to protect and provide for his wife? No, he did not. It is I who had been deemed caretaker, and provider—a role for which I was not prepared.

My feet were weary from my diligent search for work, and I was discouraged and forlorn. I wanted to go home, but I didn't know where home was. How could we have a home if I couldn't provide an income to sustain one? I longed to be rescued, but there was no one to save me. Everything was in my hands, so I had to be strong and take care of us both.

Finally I found a job as a receptionist at an office of internists. Afterwards, Jonathan and I moved from his parents' house into a vacant house his brother was selling. We had no furniture and slept on the floor.

I loved my husband, but when he stayed late at the lab at night, I felt alone. Perhaps it wouldn't have bothered me as much if we had better living conditions, but a temporary stay in a vacant house for sale, without furniture, was not ideal. It seemed that Jonathan had a separate life from mine, for he was busy in graduate school with his teaching assistantship, classes, labs, and studies. My world was working in a doctor's office during the day and returning to an empty, temporary place that had no semblance of home. It was rough being the wife of a graduate student. Sometimes I felt like crying.

Jonathan and I rented our own apartment, at last. His brother gave us an old sofa-bed, and several chairs and end tables he did not want. We bought a second-hand bureau and bed for our bedroom, and a rug for our living room. Finally we settled into our own place—for which I was grateful.

In spite of the hardships we had experienced, our love for each other had grown. Jonathan encouraged me when I had bad days at work, and in turn I was supportive of his life as a student. I loved my husband and looked forward to the little time between his studies when we could be together and enjoy each other's company.

What I loved most was enjoying nature with my husband. Several times we had been able to break away from Jonathan's busy life as a student and church layman to take walks at the gorge. There nature renewed us and dissolved the barrier between our separate worlds. We became part of the same surroundings—we could be free to kick stones, climb onto a fallen tree trunk, or trick our dog by hiding behind a stump. On the stream we could skip flat rocks across the water's surface or drop heavier ones into the deeper pools to hear them splash. We could also climb the rocky cliffs and watch the sunlight sparkle on the water below.

But the best time was when the sun began to set. We watched the pink, blue, and gold colors playing on the clouds until they faded into the west and disappeared. Our time of enjoying nature reaffirmed that there was a place where we could be equalized, where our different worlds melted away as the colors of the fading sunset that blended into the dusky blue-gray sky.

Once Jonathan and I were out of survival mode and had settled into the routine of our new life, the problem with our sex life began to bother me again. It became worse our second year of marriage; then we had intercourse about once a month. I did not know where to turn for help. When I mentioned my situation to my mother, she told me sex became less important with age. So I took my problem to God in prayer and waited, with hope, for his intervention in my life.

Dear God, I don't understand, for I did all you required. My life was dedicated to You. I attended church and married a Godly man, so why am I now unhappy? Aren't those who strive to do Your will blessed with a joy far greater than that which comes through seeking the world's vain pleasures? That was what Your church taught. I did all that You asked, yet Your promise to me was not honored, and now I feel cheated. Instead of joy, there is discontentment in a sterile existence with a love that I know but cannot feel. I cry to You, yet Your voice to me is silent. I feel alone and helpless, for I don't know what to do.

When Jonathan and I attempted intercourse, it was awkward and distressing. At first there was a problem with Jonathan penetrating me, but that was resolved within a year's time. Then there were problems with me. Inside I would feel like screaming when he would climb atop me then seem to mash his face into mine. None of these difficulties was a result of physical deficiencies; they related to an immature attitude relating to sex and a lack of experience on both our parts.

Only two times did we discuss these matters. The conversations were not really exchanges, however, but me declaring that our sex life was horrible and Jonathan listening. Perhaps he was too embarrassed to respond. I said we needed to find a solution; but since neither of us knew how to resolve our problem, the conversation ended quickly. Because Jonathan gave no input, I never really learned his view of our sex life. The fact that we could not discuss these things further, however, indicated that our sexual incompatibility was only a symptom of a greater problem that existed—a problem with our communication.

Was marriage life's cruel joke on those who were in love? Was marriage always so far away from one's expectations? Now my mind wandered to the days when life was not so harsh, and when thoughts of my beloved filled my heart with joy. Had financial struggles and the mundane chores of life worn away the happiness I once felt? Had the dream of rapturous lovemaking faded forever because we were physically incompatible? Yes, the shocking truth of reality was far different from the ideals my mind cherished, but I was too young to see or understand. Since marriage can be cruel to those who are in love, we had to guard well our beautiful memories of the time when the fragrance of romance was sweet; for our memories might be all we had to sustain us through the hardships and years that lay ahead.

3. Divorce Papers

One Year of Separation

Every step that took me closer to divorce, my whole being fought; I did not want a divorce from Jonathan. After talking with my lawyer, I knew my affidavit would soon arrive in the mail; I didn't look forward to reading it. That awful document would be another step toward legalizing the "irrevocable breakdown" between Jonathan and me.

It took two days after receiving the papers before I had enough courage to open the envelope. Since I am a morning person, I examined the papers early in the day, when my strength was at its height. It was a Saturday morning, and I was still in my bathrobe and nightgown, relaxing with a cup of tea, when I finally picked up the brown envelope and slashed it open. I saw first a letter from my attorney instructing me to sign and notarize the letter of separation. Upon seeing the actual document, I burst into tears. There on the first page was our wedding date and place of marriage— Baltimore; it reminded me of the day we had become husband and wife. We could not have foreseen then that our names would someday appear together on a document leading to divorce. Even though I knew that Jonathan and I were on the path to divorce, it was difficult and painful to accept. I wanted my husband back, and I became filled with regret for having left him and for having made a series of wrong choices that had led to this outcome.

In the biblical story of Jacob and Esau (Genesis 25:33), Jacob convinced his older brother to sell his birthright to him for a cup of hot porridge. Esau, having just returned from a long hunting trip, was famished. He decided his birthright was of no use to him if he was dying of hunger. At a time of urgent need, he made an unwise decision that affected the rest of his life.

Like Esau, I had exchanged something of great value for that which was worth much less. The price of my privileged membership into Jonathan's family was my affairs. I had relinquished my right to be associated with my husband and in-laws—to enjoy their company, support and love. This was one of the consequences of leaving Jonathan that I did not fully grasp until now—almost a year later.

I felt nervous and apprehensive. I did not want to sign the separation document, because I did not want a divorce. Instead I felt like destroying the papers. Perhaps I could delay my signing the document if I brought to my lawyer's attention my incorrect address that appeared on one of the pages. Then I might be required to send it back—which would give me more time.

"Hello, Rebecca. How are you doing?"

"Oh, just fine," I answered, although I really wasn't. "I'm calling to let you know there is an error on the separation document. I don't live in North Chelmsford."

"Oh, that's okay. We'll fix that."

"Should I go ahead and sign the document?" I asked.

"Yes, go ahead and sign it."

"But does this mean...?"

"Wait just a minute. I have another call." Attorney Stevens left the line for a moment. I had to ask him.

"Okay, I'm back," Attorney Stevens said. "Does this mean what?"

"That we can't change our minds?" I asked.

"Up until you set the court date, you can always change your minds."

"Okay, thanks. Goodbye."

•

I had almost reached the personnel office at my place of employment. Suddenly I realized I had no identification with me. So my feet turned in the opposite direction, back toward my office. It seemed as though the hallways were not real and that I was walking in a dream. Because I felt numb, I had only a vague sense of my feet as they fell against the floor; I felt surrounded by gray. My feet brought me back to my office, for my mind was not engaged.

I located my purse, then retraced my steps to the personnel office and the dreaded notary, where a very young girl chewing gum came to the counter. She had no knowledge of what these separation papers represented—my failure of the past eighteen years (marriage plus dating) and my intense pain during the last year. She was oblivious to the fact that this was documentation of two lives now headed for divorce.

After I handed my papers to her for notarization, she asked, "But where is Jonathan Shaw? He has to sign them."

Her statement angered me. Of course he had to sign them! She obviously did not know the procedure for separation: I sign the papers, get them notarized, and send them to my lawyer, who sends them to Jonathan, and then he signs the document. Of course she didn't know. She was young and had never been married or divorced. Her lack of knowledge of my situation was causing me more pain in my vulnerable state. I wished for someone else to put their notarization stamp on my documents—someone who would do it with more sensitivity and dignity. Another person, who wanted theater tickets, crowded behind me. Someone else wanted a monthly subway pass. It was all in the same category, right? Tickets, T-pass, divorce papers? Next!

I quickly took my documents after they were notarized. It was finished. I had done what Jonathan had wanted, and we were one step closer to divorce!

"Hello. This is Jonathan Shaw."

"Oh, hi, Jonathan. How are you doing?"

"I got your message on my answering machine."

I felt very calm—in control of my emotions. "Jonathan, I want you to know you don't have to worry. I have signed the affidavit. I called for moral support several days ago when I first received it, because it upset me. It took me two days to be able to open the envelope. I thought it would help if I could hear you ask me to sign the papers, because I didn't want to do it."

"Yes, I know it's hard. It's understandable," Jonathan said.

"As I've told you before, I don't want a divorce. I felt like destroying the divorce papers instead of signing them. I only signed them because I know it's what you want. You want to be free to pursue your new relationship."

"Now, wait! Let's not bring her into this!" said Jonathan in a defensive tone. "This divorce is between you and me."

"Okay, okay. We'll leave Sharon out," I said. "But when you came to visit me, couldn't you feel something between us? When you were here I could almost imagine us together as we had been for the last fifteen years."

Silence. Maybe he was listening to me this time. Maybe I was getting through.

"Just tell me, please, that you don't love me anymore and that you wanted me to sign those papers. Can you please do that?"

Still silence.

"Jonathan," I started again. "What is one year out of the eighteen we have known each other? Yes, we've been separated for one year, but when we were together that Saturday, all the time seemed to dissipate. My love for you transcends the time we've spent apart. You think we're doing the right thing, but I don't. To me it all feels wrong! Tell me, Jonathan, do you think God wants us to divorce? How do you justify this? I don't understand."

"The marriage covenant was broken," he said in his "holier-than-thou" voice.

"Yes, Jonathan, it was—but we're all sinners, aren't we? We're all in the same boat."

Oh, God! Was that all he could see from our eighteen-year relationship, after I had put him through nine years of school, moved eight times, made all his dinners, cleaned his house, attended his church—that I had broken the covenant? Then why

in God's name did I want him back? Was I not better off with
someone who had the sensitivity and understanding to see why I
had been driven to adultery?

I started again. "Nigel and Christine [our best friends] are
working out their marriage problems."

"Well, how's the weather out there?"

It was his famous "sweep-it-under-the-rug" trick. That was
the way he dealt with all our marriage problems. He would never
face them. If you don't admit a problem exists, it's not really there,
is it?

"Jonathan, I know you're trying to change the subject," I said. "I
don't want to talk about the weather. I called to let you know how
I feel about the divorce papers, and I wanted to see if you thought
you would change your mind. You don't think you will, do you?" I
swallowed a gulp of air and said, "So...well, I guess I'll see you in
divorce court. I'm really having a hard time letting go."

"That's understandable," Jonathan said.

"So...[another gulp of air swallowed] well, it'll be four to six
weeks until we go to court," I said. "I know it's going to be awful.
I know I'm going to cry. I hope you'll change your mind. My lawyer said we can change our minds up until the court date...so we've
got six weeks."

No response.

"Okay. I'll see you in court," I said. "But we have six weeks to
change our minds," I repeated. "Bye."

His words, "the marriage covenant was broken," rang in my
ears. They moved me from the sorrow I felt over our lives separating, into an acknowledgment that he was missing the whole picture of what had happened in our lives over the last eighteen years.

It was a special morning, and my best friend was bringing her *petit
ami* (boyfriend) over for dinner. How often does one have the
privilege of entertaining two people from Paris? I felt honored and
excited. I rose early and set out my china, my linen napkins, and
the wine glasses. The table was dressed with fresh flowers; it
looked lovely. The sun was streaming in through my kitchen

windows, and the blue and white colors in my kitchen looked crisp and bright. I made the main course first so it could be reheated in the oven when they arrived. Then I made dessert. Suddenly I had an urge to call Jonathan and invite him to the dinner. How absurd to call the man who was divorcing me and invite him to dinner! Only several days ago I had spoken with him concerning the separation papers and had asked him if he would change his mind about divorce. Why did I want to call him now?

I was following my heart. It was a special day, and I wanted Jonathan to meet my Parisian friends. He would like Monique. Maybe because it was a "couples" event I wanted to make the threesome a foursome. Could that explain my impulsiveness? Monique was with the man she loved, and I would be the third party—the "uncouple." Maybe if Jonathan came, had a wonderful time, and enjoyed the day, he would see that there was potential in our relationship; then we could work on our marriage. I wanted him to share this special day with me, even though I knew he would not really consent to come.

I dialed his number. It was early, before 7:00 a.m., and I thought he would be home. The phone rang once, twice, then...

"You've got J.B. Shaw here. If you leave your message and a number, I'll see what I can do about getting back to you." Beep.

"Hi, Jonathan. I'm calling to invite you to dinner today. My friend Monique and her boyfriend from Paris are coming, and it would be a nice day for you to take a ride to the country. They are coming at one o'clock p.m. If you'd like to come, you're invited; but if I don't see you, I hope you have a nice day. 'Bye." I couldn't believe I'd said that! "Hope you have a nice day." I hated that canned phrase.

Later it bothered me that Jonathan hadn't had the courtesy to acknowledge my call. But what had I expected from the man who no longer loved me? It was impulsiveness and my need to reach out to him that had prompted me to call, which emphasized the fact I was having difficulty letting go of the man who had been my husband for over fifteen years.

•

I awoke again from another dream in which I was working through the phases of divorce. In this dream I saw all of my in-laws, including my late father-in-law. The occasion was some family gathering, and I was anxious to talk with everyone whom I had not seen in over two years.

Although I was happy to see everyone, the feeling was not mutual. I saw Jonathan's younger brother, Ed, first. He looked thin, sad, very emotionless, and he was bent over—extremely elderly. He did not acknowledge my presence. Then I saw Jonathan's brother the minister. He looked younger and more handsome than in real life. He did not see me, either. The only two relatives who acknowledged my presence were Jonathan and his father. I had been seeking acknowledgment from Jonathan, but had been ignored except for a brief moment when he pushed me toward his father. I wanted to put my arms around Dad Shaw's big waist and hug him, but he backed away from me and only extended a hand. He would allow me to shake his hand, but nothing more. His eyes transmitted a message that said he would prefer to shun me and turn his back on me forever, but out of "Christian duty" he would shake my hand. It was a token gesture—nothing more, for I was an outcast.

Another horrible night. In my dream I saw Jonathan with a young woman who was younger and taller than me. I recognized her to be Sharon, Jonathan's girlfriend. We were at some school activity where there was a large building and locker rooms. I kept trying to approach Jonathan, but he was surrounded by students. Some of them stared at me; they recognized me as Jonathan's wife. Others did not acknowledge my presence. I waited for Jonathan, but he did not see me. Sharon saw me, though, and quietly stared. I was trying to talk with Jonathan, to make a connection, but it never happened. I awoke troubled, sad, and worried.

This was the second night I had had troubling dreams about Jonathan. Did they mean something? Were they significant? I decided to call Jonathan the next day and find out if something was wrong.

"Hello? Who's this?"

"Becky. I've had two nightmares about you, so I'm calling to see if you are okay," I said.

"I'm a little under the weather. I have the flu. I had to do a little traveling, and I haven't really recovered from the European trip. But...I'm fine," Jonathan said.

"I'm sorry you have the flu, but I'm glad there's nothing seriously wrong," I responded. "I don't understand why I had those dreams. I didn't sign divorce papers or anything."

"Papers? I've been signing papers too!" Jonathan said.

"Oh, great fun, isn't it?" I tried to make light of the subject. Then I asked, "Did you have them notarized?"

"My lawyer's going to take care of that," Jonathan said.

"Yes, but you must sign them first." I wanted to know if he had actually signed the papers. "Then you haven't really signed the papers yet?" I asked.

"I had to re-do my financial papers first. How's the weather up there? Is spring coming along?"

He always talked about stupid, inappropriate things! He was an artist at avoiding issues. He probably wanted to make sure the conversation didn't become intense, like the last time we spoke. Anything to avoid dealing with real emotional issues. So we talked of the weather.

"Oh, I received a note from Tanya [my sister]. She sent me a card with Brian's [her new son's] picture," Jonathan said. Now he wanted to talk about another safe topic, family members!

"She sent me a note too," I said. "Brian is really such a wonderful baby. When I was home in August, he never cried. He's very good natured."

"Well, I know it's about time for you to leave," Jonathan said. I knew he was trying to end the conversation before it had a chance to develop into my asking if we were doing the right thing. I was not going to ask him again if I could come back, so I followed his lead.

"Okay, take care. Goodbye," I said flatly as I slammed the receiver down. Damn him! How could he be so unemotional, unconcerned, and uncaring?

Then it came to me. The dreams meant that Jonathan no longer cared about me or loved me. It was painful to acknowledge, but I had to let go of Jonathan and get on with my new life. Jonathan was no longer mine. For months I had thought Jonathan's heart might soften and that he might change his mind. Every small sign of caring or kindness he had shown, I had used to fuel my hope that we might reconcile. But when my hope stayed alive, my progress towards healing was inhibited. I had to face the fact that it was over. As a result of my own actions, it was now over.

4. Reality

Three Years of Marriage

I wondered how my high school sweetheart was. It was during the spring of my life that he came to me, when the colors of youth were fresh and vibrant, and love was shrouded in mystery. He was handsome and mature—a talented trumpeter. He asked me to sit with him on the school bus, and the tingling feeling that resulted was the awakening of my sexuality. It was he, my high school sweetheart, who sent me my first love letter; gave me my first kiss, first box of candy, and first steady ring. He took me to my first prom. I wondered if he should not also have been my first lover, for it was he who prepared me with the romantic notions of what lovemaking might be. For our honeymoon, we saved quarters in a glass jar; we looked forward to the night we would consummate our love, then spend eternity together.

He was my all; I could not imagine wanting anything more. With him I felt complete, and in him was my happiness and future. He was intelligent, affectionate, sexy, loving, passionate, generous, and protective. He read my emotions as one reads a book, and the communications from my heart, he completely understood. Our relationship was one of intimacy and love. His words and motives shaped my concept of what a loving relationship should be.

Such a relationship my husband and I would never have. The

understanding and intimacy that was present between my sweet-heart and me—the desire and adoration that united our spirits in romantic splendor—was not possible in my marriage. Could I help but wonder how my life would be had I married my high school sweetheart? Wasn't it useless thus to dream?

Although my high school sweetheart never realized it, he played a role in the complicated circumstances of my marriage. He was really the only person with whom I was involved before Jonathan, so in my lack of experience I superimposed upon Jonathan characteristics that were my sweetheart's. Many times, in anticipation of our honeymoon night, my sweetheart described to me how he imagined the prelude to and consummation of our love would be. We both had been looking forward to that night in an-ticipation of beginning our sexual relationship together. Wrongly, I assumed this would also be Jonathan's view. But it wasn't. The wonderful fantasy described by my high school sweetheart years before I was married, Jonathan knew nothing about. Due to my inexperience, I believed everyone had a healthy interest in sex, but painfully I came to learn that my assumption was far from correct. My sexy, hot-blooded sweetheart's physical interest in me lay at the opposite end of the spectrum from Jonathan's.

There had not been sufficient evidence during the time I dated Jonathan to foretell Jonathan's lack of interest in sex, because our physical relationship had not progressed beyond kissing. Our kiss-ing sessions before marriage seemed to indicate there would be no problems once our relationship included sexual intercourse. Ac-cording to my mother's advice, "Beat off the boys until marriage [don't have sexual intercourse until marriage], then nature will take its course," there were never sexual incompatibilities. Most likely, for nearly everyone except Jonathan and me, this advice would have been all right. But my case was highly unusual. Even if there had been warning signs about the physical incompatibility between Jonathan and me, how could I have heeded them for a problem that I didn't know existed? I was too young and inexperienced.

Certainly, after marriage I regretted that my religious beliefs had prohibited pre-marital sex, for otherwise the problem between

Jonathan and me would have surfaced. But it was too late for that after marriage. It seemed all I could do was dream about a sexual relationship I would never have, for I had no idea what was wrong between my husband and me or how it could be resolved.

Despite our physical incompatibility, Jonathan and I still loved each other. As our relationship had not been built on sex, there were other bonds between us: our religious backgrounds, our interest in nature and outdoor activities. He was my best friend. I could always count on his sound advice to offset my overly emotional perspective. He was completely reliable and trustworthy. I loved his unique qualities, his goodness—all that made Jonathan so special. Our relationship was built on a strong foundation of spiritual love—a love that I never had cause to doubt.

How did I know of my husband's love for me? By the little things he did. He gave me blooming tulips on Valentine's Day. On a day I walked home in the deep snow wearing street shoes, he bought me a pair of boots. Earrings my husband presented to me simply because I was in his thoughts. On my birthday he gave me a bread basket for my home-baked loaves, in addition to a new spring coat. Those weren't my only birthday presents. He also made my dinner, then washed the dishes too! On a day I felt ill, he vacuumed the living room rug, walked the dog, then defrosted our refrigerator. Another time my husband gave me a red carnation just to brighten my day. These were the acts of kindness that were indications of my husband's love. These expressions of love I understood and cherished.

I had planned to drive alone from Erie to Baltimore to attend a girlfriend's wedding near the University of Maryland. Jonathan felt uneasy about asking someone to fill in for his church obligations, so he planned to stay behind while I made the trip alone. I had left work early on my day of departure, and Jonathan had met me at our apartment for lunch. There in our kitchen as we were saying goodbye, the thought of our separation suddenly overwhelmed us. Jonathan and I, clasped in each other's arms, began to weep tears of sorrow.

How beautiful were those moments. It was a tender time of reassurance and renewal, when our love felt alive and warm. This reaction to my leaving caused Jonathan to change his plans. He decided then to accompany me on my trip after all. Our love had prevented our separation, for the mere thought of our being apart had been too difficult to endure.

Another time, I spent a beautiful day with my husband on the silvery lagoons of Lake Erie, where we held hands and pushed the blades of our skates over the bumpy, slippery ice. Sometimes our gaits were in opposition, which made it feel as though we were dragging heavy weights in addition to trying to keep from falling. But the extra effort was rewarded when our clasped hands prevented one or both of us from taking a spill on the hard ice.

We saw ice fishermen and their huts—complete with heaters for warmth and cots for sleeping. Willy, our dog, ran off with someone's catch—a fish lying on top of the ice. We apologized for our dog's thievery, and to our relief the incident was taken with good humor.

In one hour's time the excitement, exercise, and cold temperatures had drained our energy, and we were ready to return to our apartment. Little did we know that our adventure ice skating that day would always remain a fond memory of a time when our love was pristine and as beautiful as the frozen, wintry lagoons.

The intensely loud sound of singing birds awoke us from our night of restless sleep. Yet being awakened by the songs of nature was a delight rather than a disturbance. The smell of the woods permeated our tent, making the difference between inside and outside almost indistinguishable. As I unzipped the tent's flap, the difference was more pronounced; outside the grass was wet with dew and the air was cooler. Inside our tent we were warm and dry in our sleeping bags.

We left our tent and began exploring the boggy terrain. We noticed trails and the tracks of other animals. We tested our tree-climbing skills by fearlessly making our way to the top as though we were squirrels in search of a new hiding place. Then we headed back to camp, took down our tent, and packed away our gear.

As we slowly walked toward civilization, we stopped at a little cemetery on the edge of the woods. Perhaps years ago a church, long since deteriorated, had stood next to the cemetery, the steeple pointing toward the heavens where the souls of the deceased were now supposedly in union with their Maker. I liked the cemetery in its present state, guarded by nature rather than by man's proclaimed gateway to heaven. If this were my resting place, I would rather hear the songs of the birds on Sunday mornings than a preacher's loud, booming voice disturbing my sleep.

After a night spent in nature's bosom, I saw more clearly the side of man and woman that was akin to the wild, and I hoped my husband saw this too. Nature was physical, with tree trunks we could hug and dew on grass we could feel. Could nature help bring to fruition Jonathan's physical love for me?

I wanted to be a good wife to Jonathan, but the standards I set for myself were unrealistic. I was constantly baking home-made bread, cakes, and pies, in addition to cooking all our dinners and packing Jonathan's lunch. By trying too hard, I made unnecessary work for myself and sometimes felt overwhelmed.

Who was I in this household, and for what purpose did I exist? I was so weary of working all day at my job, then coming home to cook dinner, wash dishes, and pack his lunch. I was tired of the routine. After my job, church work, and domestic work, there was time for little else. My workload discouraged me and sometimes whispered into my ear that marriage was a form of slavery from which I longed to be free.

I wished Sundays would never come; they were too full of work and duty. On Sundays we worshipped God. We taught, sang, directed the choir, played piano, and listened to the sermon, then went home and prepared a big Sunday dinner. We collapsed. Then we waited to attend evening church, where we sang, played piano, and listened to the sermon, then went home and made supper. How tiresome was this routine! Was God glorified, or was he bored, like me, by our dutiful behavior? I wished Sundays would never come; I would much rather stay home and rest!

When my husband was a student he was always busy with his studies, but after he graduated I wanted his free time to be spent with me. Yet his drive led him away, for his loyalties and interests lay elsewhere.

On many Saturday mornings my husband attended a men's prayer breakfast. During the afternoons he occasionally did church volunteer work: yard clean-ups, painting Sunday school class-rooms, or trimming the pastor's hedges. On weeknights he some-times attended cottage prayer meetings, church board or church financial meetings, or visited with a church friend. If my husband had free time he usually studied his Sunday school lesson or read religious literature.

How could flesh and blood compete with the Lord of lords? How could the comfort and warmth of a physical being satisfy a spiritual longing? I could not refute my husband's love for the things of God, but I despised the way it deprived me of my husband's company and him of his physical identity.

Four Years of Marriage

Jonathan finished his master's in a year and a half, then worked a blue-collar job because he could not find employment in his field. I became discouraged, because after putting him through his master's, I thought the payoff would be a good job that would ben-efit us both. Unable to find work, he applied to graduate school again and was accepted into a Ph.D. program at the University of Cincinnati with a scholarship. This necessitated a move out of state, so in preparation we drove to Cincinnati one weekend to look for an apartment. We made our temporary base a hotel room.

Why should a hotel room change the physical relationship be-tween my husband and me? I don't know why I thought it would. Perhaps because hotel rooms are where honeymooners often con-summate their love. I thought we could begin again and make this overnight stay the honeymoon we never had.

I wore the same sheer, white nightgown as on our wedding night, and imagined that my husband would suddenly take me in his arms and begin passionately showering me with kisses. But that did not happen. He was disinterested, unaffected, and non-sexual. The night only re-opened wounds from our honeymoon, several years before, when I also experienced emotional pain. I turned my head into my pillow and cried again, bitter tears of disappointment.

Why could it never be as I had imagined? Why was this part of our marriage so abnormal? I had preserved my virginity, only to have it cast aside by a husband who would rather go to church than make love to me. He had no passion or appetite—except for the things of God. But hadn't God also created sex?

There were no answers; no consolation. I had before me only that which was my reality. I silently cried into my pillow at night, for I knew the physical relationship I wanted with my husband would never be.

Jonathan and I moved from Erie to Cincinnati. Our moving day was discouraging, for we knew no one in Cincinnati. Unpacking the truck ourselves took most of the day, and our new apartment seemed small in comparison to the one we had left behind.

The following day was Sunday, so we attended the nearest church of our denomination. Although I had hoped we could use our move to Cincinnati as an opportunity to try many churches before settling down to one, Jonathan had a different opinion. Because the pastor had made us feel welcome, Jonathan decided we would return for the evening service. That night, after the pastor announced from the pulpit his delight at seeing us again, Jonathan decided instantaneously we would make this church our home. Jonathan was hooked, and since I came with Jonathan, so was I!

I'm not sure who told the music director I was a musician, but on my first day at the new church, I was asked to sing a solo. (The same thing had happened to me my first day in the Erie church.) My hope of being an anonymous member, sitting in the back row, was shattered to pieces. Almost immediately Jonathan and I were once again in the yoke of service to our church. We sang in the church choir, and I played piano in the service frequently. Soon I was asked to direct the children's choir (again, for no pay). Unfortunately, there had been little time to take a vacation from our church responsibilities, even with our move to Cincinnati. The never-ending cycle of obligations began again.

Although the church members in Cincinnati were friendly, I disliked our church, for the sermons were boring and the pastor preached so loudly that he gave me a headache. It would have been easier to tolerate if the sermons had been short. But they lasted nearly an hour. However, since I wanted to support Jonathan and his devotion to God, I put my desires aside and became a good and faithful church worker—just like Jonathan wanted. But I didn't enjoy it.

Again I had to find a job to support Jonathan and me. Since my job search had been fruitless after four weeks, in desperation Jonathan and I agreed to become the church janitors for six weeks until permanent replacements could be found. The decision was not wise, because the job involved working a night shift, which interfered with Jonathan's studies. Also, since I had registered at a temporary placement agency, I had assignments during the day—which meant I was working two jobs. Sometimes Jonathan helped with the janitor job and sometimes, due to his studies, he couldn't. One night, as I cleaned the church alone, I became so overwhelmingly tired and discouraged that I sat down in the men's room, where I had been cleaning, and cried. Things had not been easy for us in Cincinnati.

Finally I was offered a secretarial position in a psychiatrist's office, but unfortunately after two months his former secretary returned. Again I was without a permanent job. I worked for a temporary placement service until I was offered a new job as a receptionist/insurance clerk for a group of surgeons. Through this position I would meet someone who would change my life forever.

One of the surgeons in my group was also interested in piano and classical music; soon we became friends. He asked me to teach him piano, so we met at a nearby Unitarian church for his weekly noontime lessons. His musical interests attracted me, but I was also magnetically drawn to his person. He was warm and alive with creativity and charm. He understood the beauty of Mendelssohn's *Songs Without Words* and we shared the joy of playing piano. But what I liked most about our relationship was that he understood me. Since we were completely in tune with each other, our communication was effortless. It wasn't long before I fell in love with him, but I kept the secret in my heart. Yet he knew my heart!

Jonathan was in a different world; he was oblivious to many things that others were aware of—like time. To Jonathan it did not exist. During the first year of our marriage, we frequently walked into Sunday school class half an hour late. It did not bother Jonathan, because in his world we were not late.

Jonathan missed unspoken communications and the complicated nature of human emotions totally baffled him. Jonathan had no idea that I was becoming emotionally involved with my piano student, even though I spoke of him frequently. If Jonathan had observed my student's lessons, he would not have noticed the body language or detected our chemistry that indicated there was a strong attraction between us. Of such things he was totally unaware.

My husband was highly intelligent; he understood difficult scientific concepts and had a wide scope of knowledge in numerous fields. In each of his graduate programs in biology he had been offered either a teaching assistantship or a scholarship. He was also knowledgeable in history. His memory was remarkable. He easily recalled facts he had learned in courses taken years before in high school.

He was pleasant and kind and never raised his voice in anger and never cursed. Jonathan never said a negative word against anyone. He even went to extremes in order to avoid negative adjectives when describing others. Instead of saying someone was overweight, he would use the word "sturdy." How could anyone find fault with one who could not even utter negative words? Jonathan's intentions were therefore always above suspicion.

Jonathan was always ready to lend a helping hand to those in need. He never turned down anyone's request for help on their moving day or to feed their pet during vacation. He always visited members of our church who were hospitalized. When a church member faced a difficult personal crisis, Jonathan sent flowers.

He had a gentle spirit, a friendly smile, and was always willing to listen to others. Jonathan was comfortable with people from all walks of life: the car mechanic or the chairman of the physics department. Jonathan was a friend to all and had the ability to make them feel he cared.

My husband strove for the impossible—to please everyone. This meant he had to be very neutral, because supporting one side or opinion might have offended people of the opposing view. Whenever anyone tried to press Jonathan for an opinion, he would be extremely evasive. He was an artist at being indirect and private. He could avoid direct questions to the point of absurdity and could conduct a conversation without revealing any information about himself.

Jonathan rarely mentioned everyday events to me. I was always amazed when we dined in a restaurant, for only then did I learn about the things that affected his life apart from church and home. He never vented his daily frustrations to me—only to God in prayer. Jonathan kept so much inside that whenever he had vacation time to relax, he usually became ill.

He never compromised his religious beliefs. To uphold the commandment, "Remember the Sabbath day, to keep it holy" (Exodus 20:8), Jonathan even avoided buying gasoline on Sunday. His methodical personality wasn't restricted by the church's four walls; it rested neatly inside—a perfect fit. Jonathan was obsessive about church, so he delighted in following its rules. They ordered his life and maintained his sense of security and purpose.

Jonathan never dirtied his shoes with the stuff of life. He was afraid of venturing beyond his comfort zones. Instead of being excited about the opportunity to explore sex during our early months of marriage, he shied away from it completely. He would not permit himself to make mistakes that would have promoted his growth through trial and error. Instead he treaded lightly on life's path without soiling his feet and therefore did not progress.

When close friends stumbled in their walk with God (disobeyed God's laws), Jonathan had difficulty accepting it. Because it was easy for Jonathan to walk the straight and narrow his disappointment in those who failed evoked in Jonathan an air of superiority. He simply could not tolerate those whose behavior challenged his well-defined Christian parameters. He therefore looked severely upon them.

My husband was very frugal. He spent little money, and in keeping with the Bible verse "I will surely give the tenth unto thee" (Genesis 28:22), Jonathan always gave ten percent of his earnings to the church in tithe. He was also a very conservative spender and frequently monitored my purchases.

He put others before himself and his family. One day, while driving me to work after a heavy snow, Jonathan noticed a woman whose car was stuck. He stopped, got out of the car, then told me to continue driving to work alone without him. He wanted to help the woman, and he put her needs before mine and his.

Jonathan had impeccable character. He was a good Samaritan. He was authentic—too good to be true. Since it seemed he carried no evil, I was the one who ended up sinning for us both.

Relationships often compensate for what is lacking in each individual. In my relationship with Jonathan, I was the emotion for him, and he was the logic for me. In the same ways I believed Jonathan was the good for us both, and I was the bad. To me, Jonathan was almost a saint because he was so godly and naturally good. My perception of Jonathan made me elevate him and degrade myself.

Jonathan wasn't rebellious against the church, as I was becoming. He read his Bible and prayed regularly; I didn't. Even during wedding toasts, Jonathan would not let an alcoholic beverage touch his lips; I did. I was the one who questioned why we couldn't drink wine when the Bible stated that Jesus turned water to wine (John 2). Jonathan was the one who wanted to attend Wednesday night missionary service; I was the one who wanted to stay home. Jonathan always liked everyone at church, and I was the one who saw people's faults and warned they were taking advantage of his goodness. Jonathan would take no part in criticizing the church, while I constantly complained that the sermons were inconsistent and boring. Certainly, since my natural course so frequently opposed Jonathan's, I was the evil one—not Jonathan. In him was more than enough good for us both.

I had never opposed Jonathan on the issue of church before. Usually, whenever Jonathan attended church so did I. But I was becoming tired due to the burden of church work, domestic duties, and my job. Also, my personal religious beliefs were beginning to change. One Wednesday night it became too late for Jonathan and me to attend the Wednesday night prayer meeting because I had worked overtime at my job. I was glad we had missed church and was looking forward to a night off, but Jonathan wasn't. Even though the church service was over, he went to choir practice (alone), which began after the service ended. I was disappointed that Jonathan hadn't stayed home with me, but I had done what I wanted instead of what Jonathan expected of me.

Another time, on a volunteer day for church yardwork, Jonathan wanted me to help rake leaves. Although I had worked overtime that week and was tired and didn't feel like raking leaves, I went to be with Jonathan. I assisted him by holding the bags open while he filled them with leaves. After I became tired and cold, I left Jonathan and went inside the church to practice piano. This angered Jonathan, but I didn't care. The more I satisfied myself, the more friction it caused between me and Jonathan.

One Sunday morning the Unitarian church where I practiced piano on my lunch hour was giving a Sunday morning service of classical music. I wanted to attend. I asked Jonathan if we could go, but I might as well have asked to go to the moon. To attend a liberal Unitarian church would have been an abomination to Jonathan, for many Unitarian churches do not recognize Christ as the Son of God! Although Jonathan strongly disapproved, I went to the service alone and enjoyed it tremendously. After four years of marriage, I was finally developing a little independence—which I enjoyed so much that it only whetted my appetite for more!

5. Divorce Court

Sixteen Years of Marriage

Inside the courthouse, I asked a guard for directions to the probate court.

"Second floor."

On the second floor, I asked the receptionist, "Where is the probate court?"

"What are you here for?" she asked.

"Divorce."

"At the end of the hall."

"That room?" I felt intimidated.

"The end of the hall!" she snapped.

Monique and I walked down the bleak hallway. Everything looked gray: the floor, the walls, the ceiling. So gray was it all that it seemed to cover my husband, who was standing in the hallway with his lawyer. I almost passed him by; he wore a gray suit.

"This is my friend Monique."

"Nice to meet you," Jonathan responded.

Then I saw Attorney Stevens. "Did you have any trouble finding the courthouse?" he asked.

"I did make a few wrong turns," I admitted.

We entered the courtroom. Jonathan sat with his lawyer on one side of the courtroom, and my lawyer and I went to the opposite side. How odd it seemed to be deliberately sitting apart. I didn't want to look at Jonathan too closely, because I wanted to detach emotionally myself from the courtroom. Perhaps if I didn't consider what was really happening, it would be less painful. But I glanced over at Jonathan, even though I couldn't look for long. He had an unhappy expression of pain on his face, which was reassuring that at least he wasn't happy to be divorcing me.

My lawyer said to me, "First the judge will ask if you understand everything, if you believe there is irretrievable breakdown in the marriage, and, finally, if the settlement is fair."

"Who will be asked the questions first?" I wondered.

"Your husband."

If Jonathan answered there was irretrievable breakdown, I would echo his response even though I didn't believe it in my heart. Our marriage could not survive unless we both believed the breakdown could be repaired. But I knew Jonathan wanted to end it, and although I had hoped he would change his mind at the last minute, he hadn't. I knew how we were both expected to answer, for we had come here to end it.

"There will be a court recess for ten minutes," someone announced.

Everyone stood, and the judge walked out.

My lawyer went to speak with my husband's lawyer. How odd it was that they could talk to each other as friends, yet Jonathan and I, who had lived together fifteen years, couldn't.

The courtroom appeared unreal and white with pain. The walls were but sheets of paper hung from a rod, and could move in the breeze. Perhaps a big puff of wind would blow them out of place, then somehow declare the whole scene to be nothing but a nightmare.

Everyone else in the courtroom appeared devoid of pain. The atmosphere was much more relaxed than I had expected and somehow not in line with what was actually happening. I had watched to see if the other divorcing couples were sitting together. Most were. There were no tears or any indication of remorse or pain, except between Jonathan and me. Why was that so? Could everyone else so easily become divorced?

The court came to order again as the judge walked in and we all stood. The first couple's name was called, and they approached the bench. Neither was represented by a lawyer. The judge asked the couple several questions, but the interview ended when the woman asked the judge about her legal rights. He told her to leave the courtroom for counseling and return later.

The next couple was called. They, too, had been sitting together and had been chatting as friends. As they stood before the judge with their backs facing the courtroom, one could picture them standing before a rabbi, priest, or minister, years ago, saying their marriage vows. Now they were standing before the judge to end them. How very sad; we were all becoming "unmarried."

This couple also had no lawyer's representation, and I was amazed that they were laughing. The husband was foreign and apparently didn't understand the question about "irretrievable breakdown." He answered "no" when he was supposed to answer "yes." His wife had to interpret what the judge had said. Even the judge began laughing.

"Shaw."

Oh, no! We were next! We all four went before the judge: Jonathan, his lawyer, me, and my lawyer. I stood next to Jonathan as we had stood together more than sixteen years before to be married. I looked at the floor and then into the eyes of the judge. He became more solemn as he reviewed our papers. Maybe he could feel my pain.

First he asked Jonathan the questions. Jonathan answered "yes," he believed there was irretrievable breakdown. After hearing his answer, I felt numb. I glanced at Jonathan quickly, but his eyes never met mine. Next it was my turn to answer the judge's questions. I wasn't sure how to respond. "Yes, sir?" "Yes, Your Honor?" Instead, I found myself answering the questions while nodding my head yes. The judge looked me straight in the eye, then asked if I understood the documents. I nodded and answered "yes."

"Do you think the settlement is fair?"

"Yes." I nodded again.

"Do you believe the marriage has irretrievable breakdown?"

"Yes."

"Do you know that at a later date you can request alimony, if you should become disabled?" I didn't know that, but I answered "yes" anyway.

It was all over. We had become "unmarried." Then we walked back to our places and picked up our belongings.

Attorney Stevens, Monique, and I left the courtroom first. Although I was going to leave the courthouse, Monique urged me to wait for Jonathan. I stood on the courthouse porch with her until Jonathan walked out with his lawyer. Our eyes met, we walked toward each other, then Jonathan put his arms around my neck and hugged me.

"Goodbye, Jonathan." I felt it would be the last time I'd ever see him. Then the tears began to flow.

"I'll be in touch," Jonathan said.

What did that mean? We had just been divorced. Why were we hugging each other, and why couldn't we reconcile our marriage? I felt there was still love between us.

I turned away from my husband, put my hands to my face, and cried as I walked away. It suddenly occurred to me that this was a gray, rainy day, just like our wedding day had been. Was the rain pouring from the sky in sympathy to our sorrows? Was this a sign that God knew what I was going through and that He cared?

Monique tried to comfort me. "Come on, we'll buy you a cup of tea and you'll feel better."

We walked down the main street of Dedham. I was crying openly, shamelessly, as I passed strangers on the street. I couldn't stop the tears or the pain.

At a little corner coffee shop we ordered coffee and tea. Although our order was packaged to go, we sat down at a white Formica table with hard, uncomfortable, molded, plastic chairs. The coffee shop was not a cozy place, but in my state of sorrow it didn't matter. The warmth of the tea felt comforting.

Monique asked, "Are you feeling better now?"

"This does help," I said. It was odd that I was calm in the courtroom and now I was not. It felt as though my heart was being wrenched from my being. Why was I so shocked? Didn't I know I was getting divorced today? Although my head knew it, my heart didn't.

"I appreciate your coming here with me today, Monique. I'm starting to feel better now."

"Can you drive?" she asked.

"Don't worry."

We stayed long enough for me to finish my tea. My stomach felt sick, and I was weary with pain. It would be difficult to work today. The pain was not only the result of my morning in divorce court, but also from the lack of understanding about why our divorce had happened.

The rest of the day was a total loss. My boss was out of town, so I went into his office, lay on his sofa, and sobbed into the pillows. All I could feel was pain, for I ached inside and out. The hug Jonathan gave me kept coming to mind. Why had he divorced me, then hugged me? It was the only connection we had made through the whole ordeal.

It took me at least forty-eight hours to recover from that day, which I marked as progress, because it had taken me three to four weeks to recover from seeing him the previous time we met. I had thought that my letters, phone calls, and notes reaching out to him might change his mind, but they hadn't. The more I reached out to him, the more he rejected me, it seemed. Over time, each negative response from him had the effect of numbing my feelings for him and helping me learn to let go. But even after accepting that he would never be my husband again, I still found Jonathan's presence with me. For me, our spirits would never be entirely unmarried— not even by a judge from divorce court.

Over and over again I had to come to terms with the fact that Jonathan and I would never reconcile. Very slowly and gradually I realized that if he didn't want to work things out between us, then it was better to move forward without him. But it took many months of extreme anguish to come to this realization, because I had kept alive the hope that a miracle from God would bring us back together. When it didn't, I had to move forward. In moving forward, I experienced intermittent times of peace with myself about my new single life. It was during these times that my life would go from monophonic to stereo. I didn't know it had happened until I looked back, but when I did, I saw all the good in my present life, and my past seemed only a former chapter. I became happy with myself, my new home, and my friends; and I felt blessed, for my new life was rich and fulfilling, and the future no longer seemed bleak or foreboding.

Six Months After Divorce

I was driving to visit my parents for summer vacation. Their home wasn't where I grew up, but where they had built their beautiful log cabin retirement home. I had never driven there from Boston before, but part of the route was well known to me, for Jonathan and I had driven it together many times from Boston to Altoona, where his mother lived. When I came to Pennsylvania, many memories began to haunt me, because most of Jonathan's family still lived there.

The road went west, through the mountains and through deer country. I saw many carcasses by the road—deer that had been hit by cars. I drove toward Altoona, which would take me only several miles from my mother-in-law's house. As I came closer to town, I noticed the majestic mountains. They made me think of God, love, and how I still loved and missed Mom Shaw and the whole Shaw family. My heart beat faster as I came to the road that led to the Shaw's house. What would happen if I went to their house and knocked on the door?

I drove past the road that led to their house, then stopped. There was not a house in sight, but there was a tree that sheltered me from the sun. There I ate my packed lunch and tried to decide what to do. What would happen if I drove to my in-laws' house? I am often moved by strong emotions, and my feelings were intensely strong about my in-laws at that moment, because I was in their territory. It didn't matter to me that Jonathan and I had already been to divorce court and that in six weeks we'd be legally divorced. All that mattered was what I felt, and I felt love.

I decided to head directly down the road that led to my ex-in-laws' house. I wasn't sure if I'd just drive by the house, if anyone would see me, or if I'd stop in. But as I approached the railroad tracks that crossed the road leading to their house, suddenly, without warning, the red-and-white crossing gates began to close. The warning bells were clanging as if to say, "Turn back, turn back." I felt that the crossing gates were swords held by angels who were guarding the gate of Eden after Adam and Eve had been cast out. "Unworthy! You are unworthy to have further associations with your ex-in-laws, you sinner! You gave up your husband, and your right to his family. You have sinned, and now you are cast out."

Of course God wouldn't want them to associate with me any longer. They obeyed God's laws, and I didn't. God wouldn't allow me to see them or speak with them again. I had chosen to disobey God, and now I had to accept the consequences. The closing of the railroad crossing gates was all I needed to convince me to turn around. I pulled a U-turn right in the road before the train had finished passing, and as I sobbed, with tears streaming down my face, I drove away. I was an outcast. I was not worthy to see them. I had no right to love them. God was protecting them from me.

As I drove further, I looked toward the sky and saw silver clouds plotted against a light blue background. The clouds danced in the bright sunlight, and the rays peeked through the holes in the clouds to send me a message—a ray of hope. Then I suddenly felt renewed, as though a beam of sunlight had touched my heart. A voice within me seemed to say, "But they aren't as resilient as you. They aren't capable of still loving, as you are. The crossing gate was not to protect them, but to protect you! Go in peace, for you still have the gift of love."

The week before I had filled out a "status change" form to change my name at work. On the form were blank lines for your present name, your new name, and boxes to check: married, divorced, separated. When I checked the "divorced" box and wrote my maiden name as my new name, it felt very strange and painful. Today I wanted to complete another form at work, one that would change my name on the sign outside my door. Suddenly I was very anxious for my new sign to be placed outside my door. Once it was there for all to see, my divorce would be final, wouldn't it? (How many times had I wanted it all to be over—the pain and the healing?)

Next I wanted to change my name on everything outside my place of employment, so with all the necessary documents I walked to the Department of Motor Vehicles on my lunch hour. Was changing the name on my license the final act of closure, or would there be more steps in "un-marrying" myself to my husband? Upon reaching the Department of Motor Vehicles, I had to stand in line. It was moving rather quickly, and it was my turn before I had time to get my bearings. I was apprehensive because I didn't know if I'd need more documentation than I had. When it was my turn, I told the woman behind the counter that my name had changed. She looked briefly at my documents, typed my new name onto a card, handed it to me, then asked, "Does it look all right?"

"Yes...wait." I saw a mistake. "I think the zip code is wrong. Yes," I said, "it is not correct. Let me change it." The problem was the zip code—not my new name.

"Okay. Take this card, step across the hall, and have your picture taken."

Oh, no! I didn't want a new picture. I was older, five pounds heavier and I'd been through so much pain. As I walked across the hall, I heard my name being called.

"Rebecca! Rebecca! You forgot this!" I turned around and retraced my steps to the counter, for I had forgotten to take with me the card on which my new name had been typed. (Maybe I didn't want my new name after all.) I then walked to a different area to have my picture taken. As I stood in line, my stomach felt tense. I watched a young, sturdy woman quickly take the pictures. On one side of the bleak, ugly room there were several worn wooden benches where people could sit while waiting for their pictures to be developed. On this bench sat a young couple.

"Next."

As I approached the chair before the camera, I felt self-conscious. Would it record what I had been through this last year? The camera shutter snapped. I left my chair and took a seat on the bench, next to the young couple. Within several minutes, I was handed the picture. It showed a woman with a broken spirit, a woman with eyes that were sad and knowing. Yes, I looked older. All I had gone through during the past year I saw on my face. Did others see it too?

I was snacking on M&M's as I walked from the Department of Motor Vehicles to my bank. Now that I had changed the name on my license, the next step was to change it on my bank account. I had with me a copied court statement that said I could change my name from Shaw to Carroll, so I went to the nearest branch of my bank and stopped at the first desk.

"May I help you?"

"Yes. I'd like to change the name on my account."

"Oh, have you married?"

"No, the opposite," I said.

"What?"

"I'm divorced." When I said the word "divorced," I felt embarrassed. There was a negative connotation about divorce, for it represented something in my life at which I had failed. The bank teller seemed embarrassed, but then, she being older than me, suddenly became very motherly.

"You'll have to bring your court papers to do this," she said.

"I have them here with me," I said as I pulled the papers out of my purse.

"Okay. You'll have to sign some cards with your new name." She placed the cards before me. "Please sign your new signature."

Without thinking, I signed my married name.

"Oh, I'm sorry," I said after realizing what I had done.

"Oh, that's okay," the woman said with a gentle tone. She felt the emotional tenderness of the situation. It was nice to have a teller who was so sensitive. In about fifteen minutes I had filled out all the necessary cards for my name change. As I handed them to the woman she said, "It's a lovely name. You'll get used to it."

It was over, it was done. As I walked back to my workplace I felt numb. I took the half-empty bag of M&M's from my purse and began popping the little pieces of candy into my mouth. The very sweet chocolate encased in the hard sugar coating were little comfort pills for me. They were a sweet contrast to the bitter sadness of the day.

I bought a beautiful card of a woman sitting in front of a piano. She had a sad expression on her face, and her eyes showed yearning. Inside I wrote, "I wish you still loved me. I miss you so very much." Then I enclosed some foreign stamps that I had saved for him from correspondence at work (Jonathan collected stamps). At least if he rejected my letters I wouldn't feel it so acutely. I still had hopes that I could reach his heart through my writing. If we never reconciled, I didn't want it to be because he didn't know how I felt.

6. Lost Innocence

Five Years of Marriage

Unexpectedly, Jonathan was offered a position as instructor at the same Christian college where he and I had met, so he left his Ph.D. program at the University of Cincinnati to become a professor there. We moved from Cincinnati to Boston, into a lovely apartment with a fireplace, owned by the college. It was a dream come true! Jonathan had reached his goal of teaching at a Christian college, and I had gained the opportunity to complete my music degree—tuition free!

Fortunately, at the Christian college church we attended, it was more acceptable to forego church duties if one was a student or professor. Jonathan, as a new professor, was barely keeping his head above water preparing for and teaching all new courses, so he had less time for church. Since my schedule was packed with music, liberal arts courses, and practicing, I also could not afford time to give service to our church.

Unexpectedly, during the first month of classes I became very attracted to a fellow music student who, like me, was older than the other students in our class. Soon after we met we became close friends.

My feelings were enveloping me, and I was uncertain what to do. He was extremely handsome and talented, and thoughts of him constantly haunted me. When I first saw him, I was afraid to speak. It was as though I knew I would fall in love with him. He spoke to me first, but our mutual fascination began long before our first words were exchanged. He evoked powerful emotions within me; I enjoyed the sensations and wondered if what I felt was true. Should I follow my heart, or suppress the wonderful excitement that confirmed to me I was still alive and capable of feeling?

We walked to class together, and he carried my books. We designed our paths to cross frequently. I felt excitement when I spoke to him, happiness when we were together, and desire when we were close. When I closed my eyes I saw him, and when my eyes were open he was foremost in my thoughts.

One evening I spoke to him of my love as snowflakes brightened the dark sky and kissed our heads and faces with their blessing. It was an honest expression from the heart, and I, boldly for the first time since my marriage, voiced them to one who was not my husband. His response was sincere and tender—he wished he could have been the one to marry me first.

In our fantasy world I was single and we were free to pursue our love. We listened to charming music boxes playing songs of affection, we lingered at the ocean's edge, and stole kisses when no one was watching. We lived in the present, for our moments together. When he performed music for me, his passion ignited me with an electricity that jolted my being with desire. We fantasized about running away together to an island, where we would be free to love each other and plan a future together. But this, we knew, would only happen in our own imaginary world—not in reality.

My emotions for him consumed me so completely that I longed for death to free me from my marriage, so that my spirit could be united with that of my true love in an ethereal world above this physical plane. There, I imagined, we could dwell together forever in peace and beauty. In reality I could not consider divorce, for it was too contrary to my religious background. So all I could do was dream about a way that I could have my new love and God's blessing simultaneously.

Finally we could no longer carry the burden of our platonic love. Since it could not progress further with honor, we decided against our hearts to terminate our intimate, emotional bond by deliberately avoiding each other. It was a painful undoing that only increased the longing in my heart. At times I cursed our noble decision and wanted to retrace our old steps, hold him in my arms and kiss him. But that was never to happen. We had decided to do what was right. It was over; but my love for him would always remain with me—a treasure in my heart.

Realizing I had come too close to committing adultery, I told my husband about my attraction to the student. Jonathan hardly reacted, but since he always kept his emotions inside, it probably wasn't an accurate gauge of how he felt. His stress level was already high due to the fact he was a first-year instructor, so there was probably no energy left to react to my confession. A Christian couple who specialized in marriage improvement seminars had just spoken in a recent chapel service at our college, so in light of my revelation Jonathan suggested we attend one of their seminars. Reluctantly I agreed to go, even though I did not believe this was the kind of help our marriage needed. After five years of prayer, I had lost hope that our relationship could be changed through a spiritual approach.

When one is ill, one usually consults a physician. But who does a born-again Christian couple consult when their physical relationship and marriage are not healthy? Laypeople—God-inspired seminar leaders! Such a seminar couple Jonathan and I found through our Christian college.

The New Life Seminar we attended was designed to cure all that ails a marriage. The cure was simple: prayer, Bible study, and scripture memorization. Since this treatment was the same for all marriage problems, there was no need for a diagnosis! What could be simpler? There would be no counseling, no therapy, and no divorce!

Since evangelical Christians are accustomed to being condemned and feeling guilty, the treatment felt comfortable. Each person assumed he or she was the problem—burdened with flaws such as immaturity, grudges, and self-pity. The troubled were instructed to confess these faults as sins, forgive their mates of their shortcomings, then ask God to change their marriages. The transformation was to be brought about by scripture memorization, Bible study, and God's power through prayer. This was very similar to the evangelical process of becoming saved, which reaffirmed its effectiveness.

Could this treatment really change my life with Jonathan? I had been trying to fix our marriage with prayer for more than five years, and still things between us were basically the same. I decided to write the wise seminar leader about my situation specifically, to ask for advice. To my surprise, he answered with a phone call.

"But it takes sometimes ten years to have a fulfilling physical relationship. You have only been married five. Since your letter speaks excessively of your needs, it is clear to me that you are being selfish. You are the problem."

The knowledgeable seminar leader had spoken. I thanked him for his advice, but deep within it did not ring true. Ten years before having great sex with my husband? How could that be? Although I did not totally believe him, I had not yet fully developed the confidence to believe in my own instincts. After all, he was the God-inspired seminar leader. I was just a worm, so I should heed his advice.

I began my treatment, and to my surprise things did improve between Jonathan and me. I became too preoccupied with scripture memorization, Bible study, prayer, and prayer meetings to be concerned about my relationship with my husband. I hardly saw him! I began to believe that God would make everything right. I would be happy—regardless! "For I have learned in whatsoever state I am therewith to be content." (Philippians 4:11) Praise God, our marriage problems would be solved! Thank God for qualified god-inspired Seminar leaders and the healing advice they give to troubled marriages!

But the New Life Seminar approach to treating the physical incompatibility between Jonathan and me produced no lasting results. A marital problem such as ours should not have been treated as a spiritual problem. In a year's time, after the euphoric high of scripture memorization and prayer meetings diminished, things improved somewhat between Jonathan and me, but not enough to alter our relationship significantly. The frequency of our sex increased slightly from what it had been the previous year, but the nonsexual tone of our marriage that had been set from the beginning still haunted me. Jonathan was my best friend and brother-figure, but he would never really seem like my lover.

Six Years of Marriage

At the end of my second year back in school, I took a summer course on Thoreau: a fourteen-day canoe trip in Maine. Outfitters took our four canoes into the wilderness, then we set off to paddle Moosehead Lake. It was a paradise—an escape from reality. During the trip, I became attracted to one of the students.

He was strong, with broad shoulders and blond hair. He was a master outdoorsman who could catch trout in a mountain stream then cook it over an open fire for breakfast. He knew how to maneuver a canoe and pitch a tent. He had a mischievous twinkle in his eye—a warning to be on guard when he was around, for he might bend a tree branch of wet leaves in your direction to shower you with raindrops, or stretch the sleeves of your sweatshirt over your hands then tie them in a knot. I became aware of his interest in me because of his persistent teasing, which was good-natured and fun. The physical attraction became obvious one evening when we sat by the campfire alone after the others had turned in. His shoulders hurt, so I volunteered to give him a massage.

His back was hard and strong under my hands. His tanned skin was beautiful and smooth. I loved touching him and feeling his broad shoulders and muscular arms. As I rubbed his back, I experienced pleasure and became filled with desire. We did not speak. The crackling of the campfire in the wilderness night bid us linger. Neither of us wanted to let the flames die. Then he reciprocated. His beautiful hands touched my back, and a feeling of pleasure rushed through every branch and twig of my body. How skillful were his hands! I had never before experienced a back rub that was so sensuous and so gratifying. I hardly wanted to breathe for fear of distracting his hands and stopping my delight; I wished he could touch me forever. I wanted to feel his hands—not only on my back but all over my body: on my breasts, my thighs, and my legs.

Finally I became so overwhelmed with desire that it frightened me. I quickly retreated into my tent, because I was afraid of what might happen next. I knew it would be wrong for me to become involved with the student, so I left him alone by the fire as a safeguard against my strong feelings of passion.

The campfire died down with the coming of dawn, but I felt flames burning within me for months afterwards. We both had experienced desire, although we never spoke of it to each other. After the course ended, our paths rarely crossed. But the picture of his back was burned into my mind, fueling countless fantasies of what could have happened between us. Several years later, upon hearing he was to marry, I felt envious of his bride-to-be, for I knew her honeymoon would be far different from mine. Her body would be celebrated with passion, fire, and the skillful touch of his beautiful hands. How I wished such an experience could have been mine!

Seven Years of Marriage

One night, when Jonathan was away on a trip, my physician friend, whom I had taught piano, called and asked me to meet him in New York. I asked him to call me again the next day so I could have a night to make my decision. When I considered right and wrong, I knew I should decline his offer. Yet when I asked myself what I wanted, the answer was clear. I wanted to be with him. I had become the soprano in Carl Orff's *Carmina burana*, who chose foremost the experience of love.

We met in a plush hotel suite in New York City. I was twenty-nine, he was forty-two. We were each married to others, but I loved him dearly. I was Cinderella, and he was my prince—rescuing me from disenchantment, loneliness, disappointment, and a rigid, sterile existence. He understood me and my connection to music. He captivated me with his charm, intelligence, sensitivity, warmth, and humor. I was magnetically drawn to him and believed we were kindred spirits. He made me feel appreciated—simply for who I was.

How flattered and honored I felt that he had chosen me to be his companion for two days, and that I would be the recipient of his full attention. I had fantasized about being his lover before, but now that it was becoming a reality, I was not sure what to expect. I had decided to follow my heart, and tried to ignore the issue of right and wrong, but it was proving to be difficult. Yet despite my strict religious background, I selfishly wanted to seize the opportunity to make this dream come true. Didn't I have but one life to live, and wasn't this facet in the diamond of life too beautiful to ignore?

My romantic encounter with him was an escape into a privileged world of luxury. My normal Spartan existence sharply contrasted with our extravagant suite. We enjoyed not only the best in accommodations, but also in entertainment and dining. I was enchanted with the experience, and felt as though all of New York City had been laid at my feet. My prince was a delightful companion who saw to it that I had everything I wanted. It was novel being treated as a princess, and I enjoyed every moment!

Yet even as it was happening, I knew that my circumstance was not forever—only temporary. Although it was a soothing balm for the loneliness I had felt in my marriage, at the same time it only outlined my pain. I knew that the euphoric escape would leave me dissatisfied and confused, but I was willing to suffer for two days of pleasure.

Our first night together he tenderly and lovingly ushered me into the world of infidelity. Although we were both nervous, the progression seemed natural, as our relationship was already intimate and bonded in love and music. Didn't this bond give my behavior justification? Certainly if I had more than one life to live, one would be spent with my prince, and one with my husband. But since I was limited to one life, it must therefore be shared with two people at the same time. In this way, my lover and I would enrich each other's lives permanently, through our temporary encounters.

My romantic rendezvous all too soon came to an end; and my dazzling horsedrawn coach turned back into a pumpkin. But my life was forever changed; the world no longer looked the same. I felt stunned and aglow with the excitement of love. My eyes had been opened to the pleasures of adultery, and I saw colors of lavender, pink, and blue, changing the world into hues of lilacs, lilies, and blue skies. The colors mesmerized and embraced me with enchantment and delight. The memory of our affair would sparkle forever as the New York City lights from outside our suite window had that night. Only the stars would know my wonderful, terrible secret—I now had a lover!

I was alone with the fact that I had encountered my carnal nature. I had participated in sin willingly—while being aware of my actions. I felt like Eve, who had just taken a bite of the forbidden fruit: my eyes were opened for the first time to the fact that I was naked. I felt wise and damned. I waited for my punishment, for certainly I would pay a price for my two stolen nights of pleasure. But nothing happened.

There were tremendous conflicts raging within me. The excitement and romance of my affair made me long for my lover. Yet he could not be with me—he was married, and so was I. I dealt with this alone, as best I could. There was also the conflict of right and wrong. Part of me desired that which was right. I knew God's promise: if we confess our sins, he will forgive them. (1 John 1:9) I wanted God to forgive me for my sin, for I could still be good, couldn't I? After all, I carried no malice in my heart, and had not wanted to hurt anyone—especially not my husband. I did not choose to be forever outcast by God, into eternal damnation. But could I be forgiven for something that had so drastically changed my outlook on life—something which I so thoroughly enjoyed? If I saw my lover again, would I want to reject him? Could I? Isn't love a wonderful gift, to be treasured above all else? Should I embrace this love instead of run from it? One minute I desired to be on the side of right, and the next minute I wanted to be on the side of wrong. I could not decide which side to be on.

I knew what I'd been taught. The Bible said, "No man can serve two masters: for either he will hate the one, and love the other; or else he will hold to the one, and despise the other. Ye cannot serve God and mammon." (Matthew 6:24) I had served God until now. Other times when I had been tempted, I had not broken God's laws. But now I had crossed over the line.

But if I was going to be a sinner and indulge in these pleasures of the flesh, I wanted to make the most of my decision. I wanted to be a good sinner and enjoy my sins to the fullest. I wanted to be the most tempting and most desirous, skillful lover and experience all the joys of lovemaking there were, and be artful in giving those joys to others.

Did I serve mammon? No, not entirely. I wasn't completely bad; I was both good and bad. The potential for both was always there and in us all. Nothing was absolute, and no one perfect. I could not be either exclusively. I found contentment in this knowledge, for it put to rest the conflict within me. Now I knew I served two masters; I was both good and bad.

7. Breakdown

Eight Years of Marriage

I graduated cum laude from the Christian College with a B.S. degree in music education. Since my student teaching had not been the highlight of my college experience, and because I knew my husband would soon return to school, I took a medical secretarial position at a hospital in Boston. There I met a very sexy, hot-blooded physician who became my second lover.

He pursued me as Romeo; he made me feel like Juliet. He brushed his hand tenderly against my cheek, and my whole body tingled with pleasure. He caught me off-guard, then quickly planted the perfect kiss, filled with passion and eroticism, on my thirsty lips. I resisted, yet I wanted to be pursued, for the game was tantalizing and I loved playing with fire. He captivated me with his charm and eroded away my resistance—peeling away each layer with pleasure, as though he were undressing me. I wanted him to stop—almost. I enjoyed his attention, for he made me feel like a desirable woman, worthy of pursuit and worthy of having.

The fragrance of his cologne transported my senses to his bed, where my awareness lay on edge awaiting a tide of ecstasy. I was in awe of his artful skill as a lover, and became a willing participant. I abandoned myself to his leading, and in doing so experienced such pungent joy that I believed nothing so beautiful could be considered wrong. I chose the feeling of love above all else.

Our desire for each other erupted in his office, in the restroom, on his desk—a powerful movement of emotion and passion that would suffer no restraint. He made my cheeks flush with color— like the blush of a new bride. Now I had a lover who enjoyed me and made me feel physically loved. He happily inaugurated me into the new world of sexual pleasures. He taught me through giving experiences I had never before known except in my dreams.

I felt like a beautiful instrument from which he, the talented artist, could masterfully evoke celestial music during the height of pleasure. He knew when to play me softly and tenderly, and how to bring forth the sweetest timbres. He was a master at his art, knowing well which registers would produce the richest tones and how to make those tones resonate most beautifully. How thankful I was and how indebted I felt that he had opened my eyes to the pleasures of sensuousness and to the joys of being a woman. How tragic it would have been had my life ended without knowing such ecstasy.

Nine Years of Marriage

He went about his life as though everything was the same, yet it wasn't. He didn't know. I looked at him with eyes that saw the whole picture—the picture to which his eyes were blinded. I wished he were perceptive enough to know about my unfaithfulness, yet I was glad he didn't know, for it spared him great pain. He was never interested enough to explore the joys of sex with me, so weren't my actions justifiable? But he was so good, so incapable of ungodliness. Could he be held responsible for not having an inquisitive, sexual nature? Did he deserve what I was doing to him? He was so honorable—more honorable than I.

I led a double life and I did it well—without lying to Jonathan. If I told him I was going to a concert, I went; then at intermission I left and met my lover. I never lied, and Jonathan never suspected. Due to my guilt, I was more tolerant of Jonathan's rigidity, obsession with church, and high expectations of me. I continued with my duties, attending church, cooking dinner each night, doing the housework, and earning our income, while carrying the burden of my terrible secret: I was unfaithful and unfit to be Jonathan's wife.

Through having my affairs I knew it was possible to love Jonathan even while being unfaithful to him. As it was possible for a parent to love more than one child, so it was possible for me to love more than one man. I loved Jonathan for his intelligence, goodness, and for the history we shared together. I loved my lovers for the way they made me feel appreciated as a woman and because they related to me on a level that Jonathan couldn't. Jonathan was my best friend, my companion, and helpmate, while my lovers were my sources of physical fulfillment.

I looked at Jonathan with compassion and empathy. I wanted what was best for him, and for his goals to be achieved, yet I betrayed him—I was not true. Each time one affair ended, I vowed never to let it happen again, for I wanted to be the good wife Jonathan deserved. But another affair always crossed my path. It was as though Satan, who knew my vulnerabilities, placed before me temptations that I could not resist. Satan wanted to make sure I was totally his—never to escape his hold.

But maybe my behavior had nothing to do with Satan. Perhaps I was driven to this end by desperation, to fulfill my need for intimacy—both physical and emotional—since it could never be achieved in my marriage. In trying to force myself to fit Jonathan's lifestyle, perhaps I was being destroyed. Then, in desperation, I attempted to break out of this rigid, sterile existence by granting myself the freedom to have affairs. Through my sexual expression and gratification, I could obtain the feeling of closeness I needed.

I wished my affairs would stop, yet they brought to my life great pleasure—a pleasure I could no longer deny myself. I was an embodiment of conflicting emotions and values. This wore on me and drained me of my energy. I despised myself for my adulterous nature, but admired my ability to take care of my husband while meeting my needs with a lover. I didn't know how to resolve these conflicts, but I was searching for answers. Through gathering information and striving to learn from life's experiences, I would eventually come to a resolution.

•

For Jonathan to become tenured at the Christian college, he needed a Ph.D., so we moved from Boston to Pittsburgh after he had been accepted into a program in developmental biology at the University of Pittsburgh. Jonathan again became a student while I worked for a temporary agency and looked for permanent employment. Eventually I was offered a position at a hospital as an academic medical secretary. Jonathan and I became active again in the local church: the same denomination as our college in Boston. However, by this time I was extremely weary of this religion; I no longer believed in the doctrine, and I began to openly rebel.

Ten Years of Marriage

Did I believe that a person's goodness was determined by the number of church services he or she attended? No; for many good, moral people never stepped inside a church. Then why did I go? Because I loved Jonathan and wanted to support his devotion to God. But how could I be true to myself and Jonathan?

Finally I decided on a compromise for myself: I would attend church with Jonathan one week, and stay home from church the following week. In that way I could be supportive of Jonathan and be true to myself! But this idea caused problems for Jonathan. The pastor took him aside one day to ask about my spiritual welfare, which was embarrassing for Jonathan. My rebellion against the church only served to increase the friction between my husband and me.

Additional tension in our relationship was caused by my music, for it was helping me to develop independence. At the beginning of our marriage, most of my involvement was with sacred music at our church. In that environment Jonathan was proud of my musical abilities, for there it was considered a service to Christ. But when my music was not related to church, Jonathan resented it.

My secular musical activities in Pittsburgh began with singing in the Bach Choir. Next I studied voice and sought opportunities to audition as a soprano soloist. Soon I was singing in the Shakespeare Festival with a group called Goode Companie, which kindled in me an interest to learn a new instrument—the viola da gamba. While performing with Goode Companie it became clear that a separate life for me was developing—a life that Jonathan could not share. My circle of friends was no longer the same as Jonathan's. My friends were mostly other musicians—people who were not from our church. Although Jonathan accepted them, he clearly was more comfortable within his church subculture.

The more music consumed me, the more independent I became. As I allowed myself to pursue my passions, Jonathan began to feel excluded. At one point he asked if I loved my music more than him. No, I didn't. But then music's importance in my life was perhaps exaggerated, because through it I had found freedom. I had developed my own independent life, in which I could survive just as Jonathan survived in his Christian college and church subculture. No, it wasn't that I loved my music more than I loved Jonathan; I was just enjoying the freedom my music granted.

Why didn't Jonathan appreciate my musical abilities? Not everyone had talent. I could play several instruments and sing, but Jonathan was indifferent to that. As he did not understand my music, he also did not understand me. My music did not speak to him; it was an unimportant thing—frivolous and impractical. When Jonathan rejected my music, I felt he also he rejected me. My music was not just a hobby or outside interest, it was part of me. My values and goals reflected the fact that I was a musician. If Jonathan loved my music, he would understand my passions, my emotions, and my dreams. Through my music, he could know me intimately and completely—hear my heart's secrets. Music is communication; communication was the key to understanding me. Jonathan would love me more if I were not a musician, but a musician I could not cease to be.

Eleven Years of Marriage

Until Jonathan's father passed away, I did not fully understand the relationship between Jonathan and his church. At his father's funeral the little Evangelical country church was packed with church members, family, and friends. The funeral procession drove four hours to the cemetery, where the chapel was again packed with church people who remembered the strong religious faith of Jonathan's father. Jonathan's father had been a pillar of the church; every time the church doors opened, the Shaw family entered. When their local church met with financial difficulty, Jonathan's father put a second mortgage on his farm. No wonder Jonathan was so close to his church: it was his heritage. Jonathan's church was to him as my music was to me. He could not be separated from that which was part of himself.

Twelve Years of Marriage

The sexual experience I gained through my affairs helped the physical relationship between Jonathan and me improve. By this time, our sex life was normal. We had intercourse once a week, and Jonathan had come to desire me. Although intercourse now included three positions, for me it still was not fulfilling. I still had not experienced an orgasm with my husband, even after twelve years of marriage! Since it had taken so long for Jonathan to feel comfortable with intercourse without worrying about my orgasm, I was too discouraged to attempt achieving one. By this time all I wanted was to have our sexual encounters end quickly; they usually did. Normal sex had come too late in our marriage, for I had given up the hope of a mutually fulfilling sex life with my husband years before.

Discontent in my marriage was increasing, although I did not feel there was any justification for it. By most standards, Jonathan and I had a good marriage. We loved each other. Our marriage had seen hardship, but we had endured. We worked well as a team; I had been a good supporter while Jonathan continued his education. We got along well with each other's families. Even our sex life was now normal. We ran our household efficiently together. We shared a common interest in nature, and we were from similar middle-class backgrounds. We never argued, and we treated each other with respect.

Yet there was a major problem of which Jonathan had no knowledge—I was unfaithful. Underneath the calm, happy exterior of our marriage were underlying dissonant overtones on love, religion, life-styles, adultery, and expectations in our marriage. The vibrations were becoming louder, stronger. They were about to become dissonant chords that would destroy the melody that had passed between us for years.

Thirteen Years of Marriage

After three years as a medical secretary in Pittsburgh, I began taking inventory of my skills and tried breaking into a professional career. I was weary of being a support person, so I began focusing on sales. I wanted to increase my earning potential, and I would not need further education for a sales position. After convincing a sales manager at an interview that a performing musician shares common qualities with a sales representative, I landed my first sales position with a distributor of 3M audio-visual products.

Suddenly I found myself on equal footing with the men with whom I worked. This was an unusual experience for me! Although the job was similar to a boot camp for sales training, I learned the basics and after six months was offered a job as institutional sales manager for the Steinway dealership in Pittsburgh—a perfect match for my musical background. There I enjoyed building a rapport with the music departments of colleges and universities and meeting musicians at all levels, from beginning pianists to Steinway artists. It was in this capacity that I came to meet my next lover.

He was tall, young, and handsome, with thick, dark blond hair. He was enticing. His casual, smooth presence was just like the music he played—jazzy. He was confident and free-spirited, with a seductive voice that seemed to invite me to sit on his knee. The syncopation and pulsating rhythms of his music spilled over my body like bubbling champagne, and I was filled with desire. He caressed the keys of the grand piano as though he were making love, and I felt his sexual energy resonating throughout my body. I wanted him, and he wanted me. We were both musicians and players in the intoxicating game of seduction.

We knew we were destined to become lovers, yet we began by teasing each other with tantalizing imagery. Would we make love after sipping wine in a tub of bubbles? Would we suddenly pull to the side of the road, enveloped in passion, and with a frenzy of kissing and heavy, sweet breathing begin to taste each other? Maybe I would first feel him between my legs in a porch hammock on a warm summer evening. Until then we would make love while sitting across from one another over dinner, our eyes locked, our minds together, carnally engaged.

One magical night he played me inside the grand piano, my skin pressing against the comforter on the strings, with the lid slanted diagonally over us—the candlelight reflecting in the mirrored wall, while the fragrance of champagne filled the air. Together we discovered the true reason for the piano's existence, and in confirmation, it sang to us an erotic song of love, in harmony with our sympathetic vibrations. Was it real, or was it fantasy? It was almost impossible to distinguish between the two, yet his delicious thrusting inside me was not imaginary. It was one of those rare moments when reality far surpassed mere thoughts. Being with him was infinitely better than I ever could have dreamed, and I would never again view a Steinway concert grand without a smile, a tinge of excitement, and a memory of that exquisite night.

Fourteen Years of Marriage

Was my self-indulgence overtaking me? Yes, I enjoyed this freedom of sexual expression, but was I in control of it, or was it in control of me? My unfaithfulness had made me dislike myself. Had I now lost my ability to refuse sex outside my marriage? If I believed I was still a good person, why did I continue this behavior?

My first affair had begun as platonic love; it had been almost an accident. Now my affairs were not for love and intimacy, but for the sheer pleasure of sex—the enjoyment of the game. They were deliberate. Unless I could put an end to this behavior, I would leave Jonathan. It was not fair to him, and I could not continue this way. This affair would be my last. This promise to myself I would keep.

•

After Jonathan finished his Ph.D. coursework, the Christian college he and I had attended urged him to accept the chairmanship of their biology department before finishing his dissertation. Jonathan accepted their offer, and we made our final move from Pittsburgh to Boston for him to become the departmental head. Since I had been offered a job in piano sales with the Steinway dealership in Boston, I would not have to search for a job after our move.

It was going to be difficult leaving behind my friends and a job I had enjoyed, but what upset me most was leaving my lover. I had become hopelessly infatuated with him, and the thought of his absence from my life was affecting my strength to keep my double life intact.

Why did my lifestyle now include this unhealthy pattern? Why had I gone against all my religious upbringing and become an adulterous wife? I had been very religious and conservative most of my life. Why had I chosen a lifestyle in which I did not believe? Why were my emotions for Jonathan numb? Why had our marital problems never been resolved?

My pathway was riddled with questions and confusion; it was difficult for me to see and to know where to go. My vision was clouded with anger, and the pathway to truth was obscured. I began seeing a therapist to help me unravel my tangled, twisted patterns and conflicts. I realized what I was doing, but I wanted to know why.

My therapist began helping me to focus on my needs. I eagerly completed the homework assignment listing them. I was trying very hard to learn quickly, for my life was beginning to unravel and I wanted to understand why it was happening.

What did I need? What were the necessities for my life? It was unclear, for I had never focused on them. In marriage, there are always compromises and excuses for not meeting one's personal needs. I now lay aside the needs of my husband and our family and decided what I needed for myself.

My extramarital affairs showed me I needed a sexual partner who found pleasure in lovemaking. I needed the outlet of sexual fulfillment—the opportunity to express my creativity in love-making. I also needed intimacy, to be understood and to be close emotionally and physically. I needed romance—a loving relationship mingled with beauty. I needed to be desired and appreciated.

I needed to feel the fresh breeze of nature across my face and in my hair, for nature had always provided me with a renewing sustenance so vital to my being.

I needed the arts to enrich my life. I needed to make music; it was part of me. I needed to share this music with others through playing.

I needed a job to provide income to cover my living expenses.

I needed excitement and relaxation. I wanted more time for recreation, and time to be alone and reflective—unstructured time to do as I pleased. I wanted this time to include adventure and excitement—like a canoe trip in the wilderness, or a climb up a mountain, or a bike trip on roads yet unexplored.

I also needed physical exercise to keep my body fit. If I wanted to run to inhale fresh air at the water's edge, I wanted my body to respond, not hold me back.

I needed a pleasant home environment and a place that could be my refuge, where I could feel comfort and shelter from the cares and stresses of everyday life.

I needed mental stimulation so that I could continue to develop and learn.

I wanted to love and be loved deeply, and I wanted it to be more than a surface love. I wanted the love to include my musicianship. This love could not be one that only sought another in return. It had to be a love that was specifically for me, that required who I was.

My infidelities were now in the open—known to my husband. I was the one who told him the truth. It happened on impulse one evening after I had seen my counselor, when my emotions were on the surface and my thoughts confused.

Mentally I had been preparing to leave Jonathan since my last affair, for I had promised myself this behavior would stop, even if it meant sacrificing my marriage. My counseling sessions had focused on visualizing my life with and without Jonathan, so I was ready for the possibility that my life with him would end. Although I had no hope things would ever improve, I concluded that Jonathan should know about my infidelities, for only then would he believe our problems really existed. When faced with our crisis, perhaps in one last concerted effort Jonathan and I could find a way to salvage our relationship.

It was late at night, and Jonathan was still preparing for the next day's lectures when I told him I had something important to say. I was guilty, numb and callused, for I had been living with the burden of my infidelities for seven years, but Jonathan was innocent, tender, and fragile. The horrible revelation was a tremendous shock to his system; his body began to shake. He did not speak or show anger, but his face expressed intense pain from that moment on. I hugged him and put an afghan around his shoulders. Little did I suspect that those moments would remain with me forever. Never again would things be the same between us. The trust from him that once was mine, now forever lost, could never be restored.

Jonathan's solution to our marital crisis was to find a quick remedy—a Band-Aid to cover fifteen years of open, bleeding wounds. I believe he thought the proper counseling, under God's direction, could cure our problems. I agreed to see a therapist of Jonathan's choosing for couples counseling, but I had lost all hope that our marriage could ever change. I could only dream of air that was refreshing and light—free from the bondage of marriage and its problems. For me it was too late. I wanted out.

All of Jonathan's efforts toward reconciliation I did not accept: the presents, the bed-and-breakfast weekend, our sessions with a counselor, Jonathan's extension of forgiveness. For me they were all too late. I could no longer stay in a marriage without intimacy, and I told Jonathan so. He asked me to define intimacy, but I couldn't. How could I explain to him closeness, the language of music, or unspoken words between two hearts? How could I explain the joy of physical compatibility when making love, or feelings that resulted from communications so clear that two hearts became one? Why were our worlds of understanding so far apart, and how could they ever intersect? Perhaps therein was the key to solving our marital crisis. But would the solution come in time to save our marriage?

Part of me was missing; my feelings were numb. I felt no love for Jonathan—only anger. I should have felt love and appreciation, but my emotions did not respond. I cared for Jonathan immensely, and loved him with my mind, but could not embrace him emotionally or physically. When I thought of my future, he was not included. I saw Jonathan only as one who stifled my life; and held me back from freedom. He hindered me from becoming who I really was.

My anger was exploding from years of resentment of being the family provider while Jonathan was in school. He never acknowledged that he could not have achieved his accomplishments were it not for my working full time. My life had been only for him: his church, his rules, his terms. I was suffocating in his life. I wanted my own life, not Jonathan's!

My anger was hurtling through time toward Jonathan, from years past, building in intensity from its suppression. The tears of rejection that had been shed on my pillow as a bride now became torrents of rain and flood waters, destroying what remained in its path. I wanted my resentment revealed to him, and I wanted him to know that he played a part in the crisis that was before us!

My anger was pouring forth uncontrollably at a time when Jonathan was most vulnerable: when he was still newly dazed by the knowledge of my unfaithfulness, in shock that I was capable of such heinous sins. My anger numbed my heart and kept me from feeling love for Jonathan. It pushed me away from him and made me long for a new life where I could be single and on my own!

Every day the question loomed before me, "Will our marriage survive this crisis?" Every day the answer appeared to be different. On a day when our counseling session was difficult emotionally, it seemed there was no hope. On a day when I was enjoying my

musical outlets and things went well at work, I thought we would
survive. When I was feeling optimistic, Jonathan was not; he
thought our marriage would end. When Jonathan thought our
marriage would last, I believed there was no hope. The uncertainty
was the most distressing factor—not knowing what would happen. Our destiny, it seemed, rested on outside factors over which
we had no control.

Was not everything my fault after all? I was the one who had
broken our marriage covenant, and I was the one who now wanted
to leave. I was the one who was looking for intimacy, but did I
know whether intimacy was possible for me to obtain? Was I de-
manding that which I was incapable of achieving?

The sadness and turmoil I felt drained my energy and left me
without hope that my behavior would change if I stayed with
Jonathan. I believed I would commit adultery again, so I had to
leave. Overwhelming darkness overshadowed me as I considered
my separate pathway. Half of me wanted to stay with my husband,
and half of me was pushed forward by an external force from behind. It was very depressing planning my separation; it was like
planning my funeral. Why did I want to leave the man who loved
me most?

Last night the conversation with Jonathan was heartbreaking. He
said in a wavering voice, "I wish you loved me." He said his love
for me was not ordinary, and that he loved me enough to try to
overcome the hurt I had caused him. But I did love Jonathan! This
crisis was not about love. Although I had been unfaithful, it was
not due to the absence of love for my husband.

I told Jonathan I loved him, but my words brought little comfort. To him, my love was not true—the same as being unloved.
What solace could my love bring to Jonathan, since I had other
lovers? I was distraught with pain, for I loved Jonathan, but it was
useless to us both.

I could not appreciate Jonathan in all his goodness. I loved and
respected him, admired his commitment to God and the church,
but I could not accept him as my husband. He was a beloved,

wonderful, dependable friend, a platonic brother-figure with whom I had been married but had no intimate, emotional connection. Although I loved him, I could not spend the rest of my life with him.

8. Moving Forward

Three Months After Divorce

This whole month I'd been in mourning for Jonathan. Maybe it was because at the beginning of the month our divorce was final, the middle of the month was his birthday, and the weekend before, when I went hiking with our best friends, I was reminded of him. Since this month I was particularly sensitive, I suppose it stood to reason that something as simple as a bike ride would also make me mourn.

I pulled my bike from the stable where it was kept. It had been a long time since I had biked to work. In fact, it had been two years. The last time, I was married to my ex-husband. It's funny how things like that impress you when you are newly divorced and still going through the healing process. I pumped my front tire full of air. I was still not very good with pumps. I hadn't learned to take the nozzle off quickly before all the air escaped. Jonathan used to do that for me.

I peddled my bike onto a tree-covered lane, beautiful and green. Oh, how I loved the country! How I loved to see this kind of scenery on my way to work! I went by an old red-brick school house on the corner that had one room with an addition. It looked rich with history and it made me want to know its past. I smiled and inhaled the morning air. Biking in the country made me feel so alive.

Then I turned onto a road that evoked more memories. Bruce Lane passed local farms. I could smell the manure and hear the sheep bleating as I pedalled by. It must have been feeding time. I also passed Guernsey cows. Since Jonathan had spent his early years on a farm, he knew the names of cows, and he had taught them to me. I saw the haystacks for the cattle, a tractor, and fields full of crops. Oh, Jonathan would have enjoyed this scenery—a country road, and the farms.

Why was my old best friend no longer with me? He had been my biking partner, my jogging partner, and now he was my ex-husband. I became overwhelmed with sadness. I loved him still, and now I was alone. Yes, I did enjoy the ride alone, but I would have enjoyed it more had I been with him. I felt like calling him and sharing this experience with him, but I knew he was not my husband now and that there was no way to bring back the days of old, for they were forever gone.

While I was plagued with memories of the past, a new thought occurred to me. I had been yearning for my former husband, the man with whom I had shared more than fifteen years. This was the man who had been kind to me and supportive, who had said our marriage was the most important thing to him. He was the one who had helped me see things more clearly when I had been emotionally flustered and distraught. He held me when I needed to be held and kissed me when I cried. He was the one with whom I could discuss things and who had my best interest at heart. He was gentle, kind, soft-spoken, honest, and patient. This man I still loved, although he had divorced me and had said he no longer loved me. But was Jonathan, the husband I knew and remembered, still the same? The Jonathan I remembered would still love me, would be there when I needed him, and would be forgiving. Maybe he was no longer the Jonathan I remembered. Maybe I still loved the old Jonathan who no longer existed.

One night a dream reminded me how Jonathan became angry when other musicians came into our home to play music. Of course it was bothersome for him to come home from the lab tired from working hard, only to find his living room jammed with musicians and their instruments. In fact, when we were all in place, there was no room for Jonathan to go from the front door to the upstairs or to the kitchen. He had to break into the middle of us, step over instruments, dodge music stands, and shimmy between people. When I tried to warn him of proposed rehearsal dates, he usually put up some sort of resistance. His opposition was not usually expressed with words, but with looks, actions, and tone of voice. I would definitely feel responsible for making my husband a prisoner in his own home. But was it my fault he was more content watching TV?

I visited the small Unitarian church near my cottage. It was a beautiful colonial building, constructed in 1775. It had a pipe organ, and the first sermon I heard there, given by a scholarly young minister, was thought-provoking. He said that the difference between liberal and fundamental religion was that fundamentalists live only in the present. They cling to what is now, because they are afraid that they will make a mistake and lose their holiness. But the liberal religion looks forward to the future because its people know they will make mistakes and they look forward to correcting them. He also said he did not believe that one's goodness is determined by the frequency of church attendance and that those who attend every week should not feel more holy than those who attend occasionally. The point that nearly made me cry was that fundamentalists don't forgive as liberals do.

What is religion for? It's a tool for helping one find truth and for building a better person. It is for comforting those in need, and for helping them find hope. It is for enriching lives and promoting growth and healing—the kind of healing that could help me recover from my divorce.

Five Months After Divorce

I had wanted to find the hiking trails in the Skinner Woods, one hundred acres of conservation land near my cottage. The trailhead was easy to find. I stopped at the entrance to the conservation land, leaned my bike against a tree, and began walking down the path. The fragrance of the woods I inhaled with pleasure, and through the woods' stillness I sensed a great peace. Before very long I came upon a lovely spot, a hill overlooking a pond in the valley below. I became enchanted and veered from the path to a fallen tree. There I sat to view the sunlight sparkling on the pond water below and to hear the wind rustling in the leaves above. I wanted to be closer. I walked down the hill to the bank just above the pond and sat down. I felt cradled sitting at the base of two oak trees. The fallen branches around me seemed to form a sort of nest that felt familiar to me, as though it were where I had been born. For there I felt nourished. The streams of sunlight seemed to penetrate my skin and caress my heart. I felt at one with my surroundings, and I wished I could make the moment last forever.

I felt my anxieties melt away, and I began to see things more clearly. My whole life was not in complete chaos, as my feelings had led me to believe. I could see that I was exactly where I belonged. Had God found this place for me and planted me in these wonderful, fertile grounds where I could grow and blossom? In the last year there had been times when I wondered if life was worth living, but now I saw that it was, for I was experiencing its richness at that very moment. I felt strong and happy. Life was good without a husband. How wonderful to now be able to experience such great joy. I thanked God.

During the last year I had noted my dreams, for they often paralleled my stages of healing. Now my dreams about Jonathan showed no conflict or unresolved tensions, as they had before. I had dreamed recently, for instance, that Jonathan and I met accidentally at a theater. Jonathan sat in front of me. I spoke to him and acknowledged his presence. Then he became a small child, ran to my bosom, and I showered him with hugs and kisses. The next day I felt very good because I knew that within the depths of my being there was a new peace.

Six Months After Divorce

I parked my car in front of Jonathan's apartment and reached for the album of Bach's Toccata & Fugue in C-minor that belonged to him. His brother Ed had given it to him for Christmas years ago, and I wanted it returned. I walked to the door and rang the bell, but there was no answer. I pressed the button harder. No answer. I did not see any traces of light through the window in the front door, so I assumed no one was home. I began to write a note.

"Becky!" It was Jonathan walking toward me on the sidewalk.

"Oh, hi, Jonathan," I said causally. "I was returning an album that belongs to you, a Christmas present from Ed. I just saw the homecoming play, and thought I'd drop this off on the way out."

"Would you like to come up?"

"Well, if you're inviting me."

I walked into my past, up the narrow stairs that led to the second floor of the flat. The very worn, soiled, matted, chocolate-colored carpet that I hated was still there. At the top of the stairs, we walked straight into the dining room. It appeared bleak and devoid of life and color. There were no flowers on the table, nothing aesthetic, only the dining room table covered with a tan plastic tablecloth. Jonathan pulled out a chair for me.

"How did you like the play?" he asked.

"I've enjoyed others more."

"How's things at work? Are you still at the hospital?"

"Yes. I've been there almost a year now."

"And how do you get to work?" Jonathan asked. "Do you drive to Lowell?"

"No. I have a beautiful ten-minute drive through the country to the train station in Littleton. In fact, one of the roads makes me think of you, for there are only farms. One white farmhouse reminds me of the old Shaw homestead. As I rode my bike to the train one morning, the farmer was feeding his sheep."

"And how is your family?" Jonathan changed the subject.

"Mom and Dad built their retirement house in West Virginia, even though they haven't sold their house in Baltimore. The house is new and beautiful, with wooden floors and walls that are warm and yellow. Did you know Tanya [my sister] and Jeffrey [Tanya's husband] had a very cute baby boy?"

"Yes." Jonathan said. "She sent me a picture last year."

"Jennifer [my other sister] has a little girl now."

"Really?"

"Yes," I said. "She's so cute and is almost a year old now."

He seemed a little disappointed that he had not been notified.

Then it was my turn to ask about his family. "And how is your mom?"

Jonathan left the table and returned with the latest picture of his mother and Jonathan's youngest brother, who was still in college. Mom Shaw looked a little heavier than I had seen her before. Her face lacked color and softness. She never wore make-up. She appeared austere and projected a puritanical sternness. I had never seen her in this way before. I had always loved her dearly, and when you love someone you tend to see them with different eyes. She couldn't see that I was looking at her. Her eyes showed no signs of understanding about what had happened between Jonathan and me.

"You know, I miss your family." As soon as I made that honest statement, I could see a defense mechanism surface in Jonathan. There was an immediate break in the flow of conversation. As Jonathan pushed his chair back, a tight smile appeared on his face, like that of a dog that is ready to bare his teeth. His whole body seemed to tense, and I thought he might ask me to leave.

I changed the subject. "And how is the greenhouse?"

"It isn't much different from when you saw it last," Jonathan responded.

When I brought up a safe subject, Jonathan immediately relaxed. Couldn't he deal with emotional honesty? If we had been able to talk to each other about our emotions, would we now be divorced?

"I have to leave now," I said. "I promised Sarah I'd go to her party."

It seemed as though Jonathan wanted me to linger. During this half hour we had been friends amid a sea of hard feelings, misunderstanding, resentment, and hurt—all that comes with divorce. It was odd being together and sitting at the same table we had shared as husband and wife. Yet as I stood up to leave, I clearly felt the difference.

Jonathan's face showed a nervous grin. It was as though a plastic shield had just been suspended from the ceiling between us, with a sign on it for me to read, "Don't touch." Jonathan didn't want to hug or kiss me goodbye, and the embarrassed grin confirmed it.

Jonathan followed me down the stairs. As I reached for the doorknob, I looked upward to where I had installed a musical doorbell about two years prior. It was missing because Jonathan had sent it to me, yet I could still hear the melody as I opened the door.

"Goodbye."

The door closed, never to be opened by me again (or so I thought). I didn't feel sad, though. I felt exuberant, for I had tonight squarely faced the past in the present, and I felt no regret. I felt like celebrating because I had not cried and I did not want my old life back. Jonathan and I were glad to see each other, even though we did not want to renew the relationship. It confirmed for me that I had progressed further in the healing process and that I was putting the divorce behind me.

I had been using my maiden name for almost three months; but still, every time I mentioned divorce, there was pain. But I felt it was time to let my musician friend, Aaron, know of my new name, despite the discomfort I would experience. Every other Monday I went to his home in Concord for chamber music. His brother, Willard, was always there to play cello, viola, violin, or recorder with the other musicians—primarily recorder players. Aaron had an extensive library of music, and as he planned the evening of sight-reading, he took into consideration every musician's abilities. It was always a time I cherished. Aaron usually waited for me so he could carry in my viola da gamba with a gentlemanly flourish. Tonight was no exception, for as I pulled into the driveway, he appeared out of nowhere. He picked up my instrument, and as we walked into his music room I decided to tell him about my new name. I no longer wanted him to introduce me to the other musicians as Rebecca Shaw.

"Aaron, my name has changed," I said.

"What?" he asked as he looked at my left hand to see if I wore a wedding band. He looked confused. "What did you change it to?"

"My name is now Rebecca Carroll. My divorce came through in August."

"Oh."

I thought the next question would be, "Well, what happened?" for I had asked myself that question over and over again. Even as I told Aaron that I was divorced, I still had difficulty believing it myself. I had been linked with Jonathan for so many years that it seemed I still belonged with him. What had gone wrong? I tried to prepare an answer to the question, just in case I was asked. "He wasn't a musician and he didn't understand me," was one answer, but were those reasons enough to divorce? "We couldn't work out our differences," seemed a better response, but the answers I prepared didn't satisfy me. What had gone wrong? If we had stayed together for fifteen years, could it have been so bad? Together we had made some wonderful memories. Even now, to me it did not add up to divorce.

"Meet Rebecca Carroll," Aaron announced to the other musicians.

"Carroll?"

"It was my maiden name," I said.

"Was it difficult to change your name?" Willard asked.

"Yes," I said. "There was a lot of red tape. I had to get a certified court order to change my passport."

"Were you assigned a new social security number?"

"No," I answered. "It stayed the same."

"Marriage is a nuisance anyway," said Aaron.

Now it was over. All of my friends knew that my name was different. But all evening the question still plagued me. What had happened between Jonathan and me, and why couldn't we work it out? As I drove home from my evening of music, I felt the cold air full of dampness. The trees were still clinging to their colorful leaves, as one would cling to one's wrap in the cold. The cold greatly contrasted with the beautiful clear, sunny, warm Indian summer weather of last week. Then I had felt so sure that I'd done the right thing in leaving my husband. I had felt very happy with my new life, and blessed; but today, as the mist canopied the road, I was uncertain why we had separated and divorced. Were my feelings a reflection of the changing seasons?

How did I feel about love? What was love? In my quest for the right combination of its intangible qualities, I had almost come to the conclusion that the love I sought did not exist. There was no mirror image of me in thought, interests, and desires who would nurture my restless spirit. There was no one who could read my thoughts and anticipate my desires almost before they were even present in my mind. No one could satisfy my desires for romance and sex. No one would adore me. There was no one who was athletic but intelligent, sensitive and strong, gentlemanly and spoiling, musical and successful, mature but young; no one who lived in the country but enjoyed the culture of the city, who was artistic and loved beauty. No one could satisfy me the way I longed to be satisfied. I wanted someone who had an emotional connection with me so that there would be intimacy. I wanted to be understood.

When I met someone who had several interests that were important to me, the better I got to know him, the more disappointed I became. He was either not intelligent enough, or not loving enough. There was always something missing.

I did not believe in love any longer—only infatuation, the powerful passion that caused me to pledge my love and loyalty to those who could not return it. Had divorce left my heart flat and broken? I wondered if I would ever again be able to find real love. When I had thought I felt love in the past, it had not really been love at all, only infatuation. I knew now that love was not the dream that I once thought was reality.

I called a former lover, with whom I had been involved the previous summer, and asked him to lunch.

Why did I take him to lunch? Because he was so charming!

When I invited him, as expected, he told me he only had two dol-
lars, so I volunteered to pay. But I wanted to, because there are
some days when a woman needs the companionship of a
Casanova, and today was such a day for me.

During our last conversation, he had mentioned my daily diary.
Yes, his name was in my diary—not his last name, but my encounter with him, a married man, was written down. I told my diary of
our lovemaking, our passionate sessions, and our love for each
other. It was now in the past, although the memory and the attraction were still alive. He asked me about my diary because he was
extremely paranoid about being discovered. Perhaps he thought
someone reading my diary might expose him. But the likelihood
of that was very slim. There was a much greater chance that he'd
be caught by his own carelessness.

Where could we go for lunch? He suggested a pricey, intimate
place, and I agreed with his choice. We met at the restaurant and
were first seated near the window. He said he wanted to move because the sun from the window was hot, but I knew the real reason: he didn't want to be seen. We moved to a safer spot and each
ordered a glass of chablis. Our eyes met from across the table and
relayed messages of excitement, passion, and desire. Yes, it felt like
we were sixteen, wildly in love and made for each other.

We talked about love, and we said we loved one another, but I
don't know that it was really true. If we changed our circumstances
and were together forever, wouldn't the fascination decrease?
Wouldn't the passion diminish? Wouldn't we then be like every
other couple, wishing for someone else? Didn't every married
couple start with the same unending love? Yet it was fun to believe
in the ideal—the ultimate love. It was an escape to hold this delight within one's heart for even so short a moment. So wasn't it
right to relish this fascination? Was there anything in life better
than this?

We followed the dynamics our emotions directed and spoke
sensuously to one another. We said we had never had comparable
lovers and that we were truly in love. But I don't know that it
was really true. His powerful desire started a crescendo that

transported me into another realm. I was sensitive to every nuance of affection that was offered to me as I abandoned myself in the beautiful melody we played that wove an intricate counterpoint. Abandon is familiar to musicians, for as they become absorbed in the bars and phrases of music, the sound, if it's perfect enough, and if it strikes resonating chords in the heart of the listener, seduces and transports the player into a blissful experience. We both were musicians, and perhaps that's why the spiritual link was so powerful. And so we performed the duet of love together, deliciously enjoying each moment, carefully feeling the rhythms and pulses as our hearts pulled each other toward unity. Wasn't it wonderful to think that this experience was unique and could only happen between us?

Before, I would have fallen hopelessly in love; but now I knew better. So why, if I no longer completely followed my feelings, did I drink in this experience, not wanting to control it, but to let it control me? Why had I asked him to lunch and become captivated by the passion and emotion? Because I was fascinated by the splendor of romance!

The mail waiting for me after my return from Thanksgiving vacation did not look very interesting. I shuffled through the letters, advertisements, and newsletters. Wait! There was a small envelope addressed in my ex-husband's hand. What message would there be from the man who had once been my husband? It was probably my monthly check, and since last month he had written a little note, maybe he had done so this time too. I quickly ripped open the envelope. The jagged edges left a large scar instead of a neat slice. A check was enclosed, with a letter that stated that this was the final remaining balance for five months owed on the pension settlement.

That was it. Jonathan's obligation to me was over. He had paid me off, and now I was out of his life forever. There would be no more monthly checks and no more notes. I was on my own. Another layer of closure had taken place in my divorce, and it made me feel sad.

"Thank you for your note," is all he said. I had written him a message last month that left the doors open between us; I had invited him to visit me. His only reply was the one I received today, that acknowledged receiving my note. Receiving his note and final check made me feel that there was no hope of reconciliation.

At times when I felt this way, good memories of our marriage plagued me. I remembered when we walked in the woods together in Erie, Pennsylvania with our dog, Willy. There was one spot where a tree had fallen, and while the trunk was still on the ground, the top of the tree rested in the branches of other trees, which allowed the trunk to be a plank one could walk, with a twenty-foot drop on either side. Jonathan was always braver than I, and he would walk on the trunk all the way to the end, and then help me come out with him. On this fallen tree, he carved our initials together in a heart. The carved initials probably still remained, even though our relationship was now over.

That night when I crawled between the sheets in my bed all alone, I could remember only the good things about Jonathan and our marriage, and that made me miss him even more. The cottage where I now lived alone seemed to echo my loneliness. Even when two people are not engaged in the same activity while in the same house, they are not alone. There is a presence and an awareness of each other. I realized then that I missed being married.

As tears streamed down the side of my face, I asked God what had happened, why we were divorced, and why we could not work out our problems. There was no answer. How cruel life was, and how it played tricks on us. When I was with Jonathan, I longed for freedom and longed for the chance to be myself. When he was my husband I loved him, but I didn't appreciate him. Now, as our divorce was final, I knew that I should have tried harder to be happy with him and with circumstances as they were. Now there was no chance of reconciliation. Now it was over, and now I felt all alone.

9. Leaving

Separation After Fifteen Years of Marriage

I cried because I couldn't believe I had left Jonathan. My leaving seemed like a startling surprise that I had no idea was coming; yet I had planned it for months. Could I not have known this would be the result? Our last night together we sat on the sofa together watching "Masterpiece Theater" while we ate pizza—our usual routine. It felt both sad and strange, for all the while I knew I was moving out. I began to miss him while we were still together, and the thought entered my mind to call off my move. But I didn't. An unknown force kept pushing me from behind. Today, before I left Jonathan, we cried in each other's arms. I didn't want to leave him. Yet I did. Part of me was numb, otherwise I could not have done it. By leaving, I wanted to see if I could shock my numbness back to life, see if the drastic move would register the emotion and feeling I had lost for Jonathan.

The first two hours after leaving, I felt a euphoric surge of excitement—happiness that I was finally free. But it was temporary. Later, when I went to bed on my roommate's sofa, I cried myself to sleep. What I had done was beginning to register.

Jonathan's brother called me at work to say he had received a four-page letter from Jonathan that had been sent to everyone in his family, about my infidelities. "Well, it's been nice knowing you," my brother-in-law said to me in closing. I felt I had just been dismissed from Jonathan's family, and in reality, that was true. After receiving his call, I ran into the restroom to vomit. Four days after beginning our trial separation, it seemed the outcome had been determined. The bridges to my husband's family had been burned.

When I moved out, my feelings for Jonathan were only pushed further away from me. Distractions of other men and my new-found freedom prevented me from becoming in touch with my emotions. I was still numb.

I wanted to press a hold button on my marriage while pursuing my love interests apart from Jonathan, and in my own way try to uncover the answer to why I had been unfaithful. I thought Jonathan would patiently wait for me—give me time to experiment. But how long could I realistically expect him to do so?

I was illogical; the stress of the past six months had left me totally without reason. Since I was not in touch with my logic or feelings, I was ungrounded and lost. I was pursuing my new life without recognition of what I had left behind.

Two Months of Separation

When Jonathan came to visit earlier this month, I enjoyed his company. Being together again made me consider going back with him. It felt familiar. The novelty of living in this house with a roommate had worn off. I was tired of rooming with someone else and not having a place of my own. It was difficult to make ends meet, and the bills were accumulating. It was depressing. Yet I was still so confused. One minute I wanted to go back to Jonathan, and the next minute I was sure my marriage should end. After his last visit, I cried. I felt lonely when I lived with Jonathan, but the loneliness I felt now without him was worse.

I was vulnerable and confused when he came into my life, this married man with persuasion and charm. I remember clearly the first time I heard the sound of his voice, for it stirred my heart. I did not know him; I had never seen him before, yet his voice seemed familiar. Within several months, his interest in me became obvious. His proposition was clear and direct, but my refusal only added sport to his game. In my weakest moments, he was there; when I was lonely and depressed, he was there, always chipping away at my resistance until I began to miss him when he wasn't nearby.

He took me to an expensive restaurant for lunch, then asked if he could hold my hand under the table. One night we drank champagne in the park, then he kissed me. Soon I wanted him as much as he wanted me. He retreated—long enough for my wanting to increase and for the spell of romance to take possession of my being. At the precise moment my longing reached its greatest intensity, he became my lover. Against the soaring music of Vaughan Williams, he promised to carry out any fantasy my heart desired. His mission was to bring me pleasure and satisfaction.

Together we entered a world of illusion in which I had no impending divorce and he was not burdened with the responsibility of a family. We were two storybook characters: a damsel and a knight. We made love on his cloak by the light of the sun and moon. He lifted me high upon his horse of delight, and I rode with him to mountainous peaks and then silvery clouds. The mist on my face, the celestial music and the aroma of incense mingled with wine, granted our lovemaking enchantment and magic. The spell lasted for days and was renewed by each fresh encounter. But the dragon of reality was stronger than my lover's steed, and our fantasy soon vanished into the sky.

The drop from silvery clouds to the depths of despair was dramatic and devastating. My knight was a married man with a family; he went back to his real life, for that was where he belonged. I went back to my real life of separation, confusion, and loneliness. The beauty and romance of our affair changed to agony and pain. The mist that had obscured from view the bridge between fantasy and reality lifted. I could not have both fantasy and reality. My choice of fantasy had left me now alone.

Three Months of Separation

Jonathan had been in my office. There was evidence of his visit on my desk: mail from home and a hand-written note that asked if the most loving thing to do would be to close the relationship. When confronted with these words, I became upset and bewildered. During his last visit, in June, we had agreed to stay separated three more months, see each other more frequently, then move toward reconciliation. But his note indicated a complete change of heart, which made me feel disappointed and distraught. Although I had wanted to remain separated until I could understand my obsession with romance and love, I saw that Jonathan was withdrawing from me. I would soon have to ask if I could move back in with him, even though the timing wasn't yet right for me.

I was honestly, in my own way, searching to find the answer to why I had gone astray in my marriage. I did not realize then how important time was in uncovering the truth. My tendency, in desperation, was to rush the process. I wanted a quick answer that would point to a solution that would save my marriage.

I was trying to diagnose and treat myself, since I was not seeing a counselor, by reading everything I could find about divorce and relationships. One could tell the book I was reading by noting the latest dysfunctional label I had tagged myself with. In almost every case study encountered in my reading, I saw myself, which further convinced me I was at fault for the failure of my marriage.

One day I saw a program on television about sex addicts, so I bought the book *Love and Addiction* by Stanton Peele. I wanted to investigate the possibility that I might be a love addict, so I sent away for information about Sexual and Love Addicts Anonymous (SLAA). This was an organization similar to Alcoholics Anonymous that tried to help stop a pattern of sex and love addiction in its members' lives. They drew on four resources for recovery: one's own willingness to stop the behavior each day; supportive fellowship through SLAA; use of a twelve-step recovery program; and a relationship with a higher power for strength to aid in recovery. According to their forty self-diagnostic questions, I had many symptoms of a sex addict, so I decided to attend one of their meetings.

My first impression was that the meeting reminded me of an evangelical Christian prayer meeting, where people informally share personal struggles and triumphs in their lives. Each person at the SLAA meeting stood and addressed the group. It began with an introduction in which each person stated his or her name, then said, "I am a sex addict." Next, each verbally vented the temptations he or she had faced during the week. One confessed to seeing a "dirty movie," and another had difficulty ending a destructive relationship.

Then it was my turn. I told everyone my name, but I could not say, "I am a sex addict." Although I thought it was possible, at the moment of my introduction I had doubts; I was not one hundred percent sure. I told everyone about my extramarital affairs and how they had led to the destruction of my marriage. Then I sat down. At the end of the meeting I did not feel any closer to understanding the events that had led to my marital crisis. However, I decided to try one more meeting to be sure. After the second meeting, I never returned.

Initially I had wanted to use the fact that I had attended a SLAA meeting as tangible proof to Jonathan that I was trying very hard to make myself better. I thought it might persuade him to take me back. But when I saw that nothing was changing his mind about filing for divorce, the immediate need to find answers decreased. I still continued to search for answers, but in my own way, in my own time.

We met in the apartment where we had once lived. The air was chilly—the walls within held no warmth. It was not a home, just a place—sterile and uncordial. The chilly environment reflected Jonathan's attitude: stern, and unforgiving. Our meeting began as a lecture that covered things he'd learned since our separation. In a cold voice, he said he could live alone, without me. He told me that other things in his life were important, such as friends and his faith. The breath from his words froze in the air before me. The relationship we had had during our last meeting in June no longer existed. My stomach coiled in knots, and my being shivered with rejection.

Surely if I placed before him evidence of my searching, he

would see that I was trying to seek answers. I had attended a SLAA meeting; didn't that prove something? Even though I had not been able yet to overcome my vulnerability to romance and love, I was trying.

His negative words left me totally defenseless. That freezing night, he spoke to me of divorce. I left his cold apartment seeking warmth, but the chill never left me.

Once Jonathan rejected me, my feelings for him returned. It was the shock-effect I had sought when I moved out. I decided I wanted to move back in with him, even though I had not been healed. Although I had not totally convinced myself I was a sex addict, I did believe I was a malignant, unhealthy person who had single-handedly destroyed my fifteen-year marriage. I doubted everything in my life, including my decision to tell my husband that I had been unfaithful and my decision to leave him. But now that I again felt love for him, I wanted a new chance at reconciliation.

But Jonathan's words of divorce stayed with me. All the next day hot tears flowed from my eyes as I tried to contact my husband to ask if he would let me return. Separation had felt safe. I thought I could return to the life I had left behind. But divorce was final, and I had begun to realize that I didn't want to close the door on my life with Jonathan forever.

I left a message on Jonathan's answering machine that I wanted to move back. Then I called again from the train station on my way home. This time he answered the phone and sounded very stern. He said there were some things he felt very strongly about, and that he would meet me at work tomorrow. He did not say what his strong feelings were about, and he did not say whether or not I could move back.

In desperation, I made a frantic attempt to turn the tide against our probable divorce. Although none of my previous attempts at using my religion had worked, I turned again to God for help. I called my mother to ask if she would support me in prayer at the precise time Jonathan would visit my office. She agreed. She also asked her church and my sister to pray for us.

Jonathan came to my office the next morning. For the first time since our marital crisis, I saw him cry. It was only at this outpouring of his emotions that I became aware of his pain. Although I again brought up my efforts at uncovering the root of our problem and said I would do anything to have him back, he was firm in his decision to divorce me. It was now his turn to be angry. There in my office he divided my world from his by separating me from the people of his Christian denomination—those, he reminded me, whom I had detested. It was me against Jonathan and his Christian college community, who he said loved him most and treated him better than I did. As Jonathan left my office, I knew then it was over.

I cried, for I believed my pain was well deserved. I had been unfaithful, and had left my husband. I should not have done so. Certainly Jonathan deserved someone who would treat him better than I did. He would be much happier without me, so why should I cry? Divorce was best for Jonathan! As if to seal the fate of our meeting, upon returning home that evening I received a letter from my husband that told me he had met another woman who had become a "healthy friend." His only closing was, "I'll be in touch."

Four Months of Separation

What pain, irony, and agony to now have my feelings for Jonathan emerge in such vividness and brilliance. To not have felt my love for him, and now to have it magnified before me at a time when it was too late—was not this cruel fate suitable punishment for my sins?

This time I could not say it was for love. I had not known him long enough. We had gone to lunch several times on business, and I found him attractive. He had a beautiful profile and wavy, brown hair, with olive skin and hazel eyes. He had a sense of humor, was quick-witted, career-driven, and was looking for blocks of pleasure that could be wedged between his long hours of obsessive work.

I was separated, vulnerable, lonely, and depressed. My husband was filing for divorce; I had nothing to lose. But I didn't want to be involved with a married man again. He asked me to go with him to the beach; I refused. He said he would leave his genitals at home. Then he asked me to accompany him on a business trip to Las Vegas. Again I refused, but he would not give up. He called a third time and said he'd reserved plane tickets for us. Then he asked me to give him 278 reasons why I could not accompany him. I laughed. On his fourth call, I gave in.

How would it be to spend a weekend with someone I hardly knew? I felt nervous, but enjoyed the surge of excitement that resulted from fantasizing. I liked him and knew we had fun during our business lunches, but would we be compatible lovers?

I had never been to Las Vegas before. Lights, glitter, and slot machines were everywhere. Our hotel suite was extravagant, with a giant Jacuzzi, king-sized bed, and mirrors on the ceiling! Initially, I was so nervous that I drank too much champagne, but it did not inhibit our lovemaking. We continued through the early hours of the morning, to the soft light of candles and fragrance of incense. He was so tender and gentle with me that I could almost have mistaken it for love.

The next morning he wanted a better room, so we moved to a suite that was even more magnificent than the first—with a glorious view of the swimming pool many floors below. It was spacious and full of light, also with a king-sized bed and an elaborate Jacuzzi framed by drapes from the ceiling. The suite was beautifully furnished, and the colors were light and accented with gold.

I was the woman he had brought solely for pleasure; I was his playmate and escort, and in return for his gratification, I was pampered in luxury. While he attended business meetings, I enjoyed my extravagant surroundings and relaxed at the pool.

In the afternoon we drank piña coladas by the pool. In the evening we dined at expensive restaurants and attended shows, but every activity was secondary to our interludes of lovemaking. My most beautiful memory of our weekend is an image of his olive skin against mine, reflected in the mirrored ceiling, our limbs entwined.

He whispered to me lover's secrets. I chuckled at learning of his sexual encounters with his college girlfriend, in his dorm room on a bunk bed above his roommate. I listened to his description of *ménage à trois*. Conversations like these do not usually happen between husband and wife. I could listen impartially, without jealousy or judgment, as an equal player in the game of adultery.

One morning, as in the movies, we ordered breakfast in our room. A table was rolled in, dressed with a crisp, white linen cloth, and I saw plates that were domed with silver. Later that evening he played blackjack with me on his arm; I felt glamorous, even though my evening dress had no sequins.

Although we didn't share many common interests and our backgrounds were very different, our time together had been rewarding. By the end of our lovers' retreat, I could feel myself wishing for more than just a temporary encounter. I had become very fond of him. He could tell I was wrestling with the meaning of what had just taken place. He told me to remember our encounter of pleasure as though it were frozen in time—having no relationship to that which was before or after. This was difficult for me to do, for all of life was related to that which precedes and follows. Even my marriage began with a wedding, and it would end with a day in divorce court.

Was not this affair also part of life? No. It was not. Our time together in Las Vegas had no beginning; we barely knew each other before the trip, so there was no history between us. The only relationship we had was that which we developed during our retreat. The temporary pleasure that transpired between us was frozen in a block of time. There would be no relationship afterwards—no comfort, no love. I would face my divorce hardships alone. "Frozen in time" meant I could not depend upon him for anything; I was alone.

A small block of ice in the vast, rough sea of divorce, was my lovers' stay in Las Vegas. It dissolved into the dark waters of my troubled life, leaving no trace of its existence in the waves of loneliness and pain.

I felt like a total failure in every aspect of my life. I spoke with the management at my place of employment and asked for an increase in salary, because without Jonathan's income, I could not survive. I thought they would meet me halfway, but I was wrong. Instead, I was out of a job. I no longer had an income or a husband.

My nightmare became a reality, for I packed my remaining belongings at Jonathan's apartment, and moved them to my place. I had had bad dreams about this for five days, because this dreaded chore meant divorce was inevitable. I did not want to drag out the pain of uncoupling, so I decided to make my final move with courage and haste. It left me crazed with pain, as turbulent emotions filled my confused, distraught being. I did not know what I was doing as I sorted through my childhood treasures, formal gowns, hair curlers, and books, throwing most of these things in a pile for the Salvation Army. There was an urgent need to streamline my life and to do without, now especially since my husband and I would never reconcile. I wanted to throw everything away, perhaps because I felt I had also thrown away my marriage.

My mind was blurred as I packed the final boxes. I had resolved to be composed and collected, as though I did this every day, but the façade did not continue very long. When Jonathan held my hand as he blessed our lunch, my tears began to flow. Everything about the day felt wrong—and so I cried.

I cried as the packing continued. I hugged Jonathan around the waist and asked him if we were doing the right thing by proceeding with divorce. He replied, gently but firmly, that we were. I knew his response meant we would never be together again, and that our life as we once knew it could never be recaptured. Gone were the days we had shared as husband and wife, and gone was my husband's love for me.

Although we had been separated five months, it had always seemed temporary—as though our marriage could still be recovered, because nothing had been resolved. But now that there was to be divorce, it felt like our marriage was over. Moving the rest of my things from Jonathan's apartment brought into the forefront a persistent pain of divorce that would haunt and torment me for years.

I missed Jonathan immensely. If the clock's hands could only be turned back to the hour I left him on April 2, I would not have moved out. Things looked and felt differently now since Jonathan had withdrawn his love. Isn't it odd? Now I couldn't recall the things about Jonathan that were so hard to tolerate.

Always present was the pain of divorce—never ending, ever persistent, robbing me of sleep and peace. To cope, I found it best to force thoughts of Jonathan from my mind. This helped to ease the ever-present, throbbing pain within me.

What I found most difficult to comprehend was how Jonathan had suddenly eradicated fifteen years of love for me. Although I experienced a period of numbness when my feelings of love for him were lost, my love was still there. But Jonathan had completely turned off his love for me, as one turns off a faucet. This I could not comprehend. I wished I could, for understanding and truth helped to ease the hurt.

Since divorce was inevitable, I decided to look for an apartment of my own, because having a roommate was difficult. I desperately wanted a private place where I could heal. I found a wonderful little cottage that was perfect for me, overlooking a meadow in Groton. Luckily, the landlord believed I would be a good tenant, even though I was between jobs. I couldn't wait to move in.

I had nothing to put into my three-room apartment except a futon, one borrowed bureau, a piano, a harpsichord, and my viola da gamba. I had not realized how expensive it would be to start over. But I was so happy to be on my own that I was willing to live without furnishings until I could afford to buy more. I knew I would survive, and I loved my new place so much that I thought I would stay forever!

Six Months of Separation

I needed comfort from my lovers. They helped to ease the pain, temporarily, by making me feel loved. The interludes of pleasure were a welcome relief from the loneliness of my reality. When I was rejected by my husband, as I was yesterday, my instinctive reaction was to seek comfort from those who appreciated me—my lovers. They would soothe my aching heart, caress my body gently, and kiss me tenderly. They would quench my longings and make me feel desirable.

The behavior was instinctive. As one who is stressed reaches for chocolate or relaxes with a glass of wine at the end of a rough week, the behavior was reactionary. What I did to ease my pain during separation was no different from when my husband and I were together. It was the pain of an unfulfilled love that had driven me to a lover; now it was the pain of rejection. As they had eased my pain before my separation, so my lovers eased my pain afterwards.

I met with my lawyer for the first time today. I had been dreading the meeting because it was another step closer to divorce—which I was against. Attorney Stevens was kind, warm, and caring. I was at a loss for what to say when he asked what had gone wrong in my marriage. I asked myself the same question. I did not know. Was it my unfaithfulness? Was the failed marriage all my fault?

Attorney Stevens could not understand why I was not asking for compensation, since I had supported my husband through a Ph.D. But in my guilty state, I could not. How could I ask to be paid for all the pain and tribulation I had caused my husband? I felt so badly about how things had turned out that I could not think of asking for alimony. I felt that I deserved very little.

My visit with my lawyer was not the horrid experience I had expected, because he was kind in spirit. Kindness meant so much during a time when my whole world had fallen in shambles around me.

Divorce was loneliness. It was leaving my mate behind and starting over—from the very beginning. The loss was not one relationship, but many, including family and friends. In-laws rallied to the side of their loved one, and coupled friends vanished, because it was too painful for them to relate to you as a single person. Friends did not want to take sides. Divorce meant building a new support system from the beginning. It was starting over as though I had no history.

My emotions fluctuated erratically between extremes. I went through periods when I missed Jonathan terribly. Then I suddenly felt happy that I was living in the country, in my own cottage. I went through periods of sadness, depression, and loneliness, then I felt contentment. Frequently I cried—especially when I thought that Jonathan and I would be divorced.

I noticed more pain after Jonathan communicated with me. My emotional mood-swings became wilder, and I switched into a reactionary mode, losing all sense of logic. I felt lonely, depressed, sad, and guilty. Because my husband no longer wanted me as his wife, I felt insecure and worthless. I was confused and bewildered about being separated and on the road to divorce. Regret consumed me, as did the desire to try to explain to my husband how and why we had reached our crisis. Yet how we had reached our state, I did not know, myself.

Seven Months of Separation

I didn't realize at the time the additional stress I had put on myself by changing jobs. I had been employed as a consultant for six weeks after quitting my piano sales job, when I decided the temporary job was not a good match for me. I then applied for a medical secretarial job because I was so emotionally distraught due to my divorce that I felt I could no longer do sales. It had been as a secretary that I had supported my husband during most of the time he was in school, so it felt comfortable.

Being unemployed again confirmed that my life was a disaster. I felt so distraught that for a fleeting moment the thought of ending my life crossed my mind. I felt incompetent and unable to take care of myself. This reinforced the feeling that I had ruined my life by leaving Jonathan.

Eight Months of Separation

Until this point in my separation, my relationships and affairs had been escapes from the stresses of a marital crisis, and mostly for comfort and pleasure. Now that divorce was inevitable, I wanted to be part of a couple again. I asked a fellow I had met folk dancing to a local contra dance in Groton. He accepted the invitation, and a six-week relationship resulted.

I knew Scott was not a perfect match for me, but he was also going through a divorce, so we had that in common. We both enjoyed dancing and hiking, and we did have fun together. I was very vulnerable, and without realizing it I began to cling to Scott because I was needy. I overlooked our obvious incompatibilities and decided I loved him because it felt comfortable. At Thanksgiving I embraced his family, perhaps because they represented the in-laws I had lost. It felt normal to be in a family again, and I enjoyed the false impression that I belonged. I was now very aware of the good things about marriage that I had taken for granted and now missed: being part of a couple and belonging.

Scott was a year ahead of me in his divorce. He had also been at the needy stage a year before me. His girlfriend at that time had ended their relationship for that reason. Although he mentioned this to me, I did not recognize myself as being in that state. A few weeks after Thanksgiving we were supposed to meet at a dance, but he canceled our date over the phone. I had felt him withdrawing from me, so I asked if it was over between us. He responded that it was, and our affair ended as quickly as it had begun.

The break-up was especially devastating to me because it made me feel like a total failure. Not being able to keep a steady relationship only confirmed it. I had reached the lowest point of my life. I felt undeserving of love, happiness, and almost life itself.

10. The Finale

Eight Months After Divorce

Why it happened that day I'm not sure, for it hadn't been planned; but then I am impulsive and often guided by my emotions. It had happened in my mind many times before that day, so perhaps I wanted to make it a reality.

I glanced at my cottage before I left. It pleased me. The furnishings, which I had chosen myself, had been placed to bring out the most beauty in the room. It gave me a positive feeling to look at the lovely home I had created myself, all alone. I loved my cottage and its setting, for it was an extension of me and it was special, for this was the first place I had lived on my own alone. I felt blessed, and this blessing I took with me as I left.

I was excited as I began to drive east. The thought of seeing him again made me feel contented. I began to rehearse in my mind what I would say. I wanted to ask all of those questions that plagued me. But what if he wasn't home? Maybe he was still on his skiing weekend. No. Today was school. He'd have to be there to teach. I trusted my instinctive feeling that all would go well.

The closer I got to Plymouth, the more heavy the traffic and the darker it became. I hoped it would be night when I arrived, because I didn't want anyone to see me. It seemed to take forever to get to his street. As I approached the apartment I hoped to see lights on indicating he was home, but as I drove by I saw

that the apartment was dark. Then I drove to the parking lot to
see if his car was there. Yes, it was! So I decided I'd pull in front of
his apartment and wait. I drew the hood of my coat over my head
so that no one passing closely by the car would recognize me.
Then I just sat. It became colder and darker. I drew my hands inside the coat sleeves and pulled my hood tighter. Every so often I
would flip on the ignition and look at the dash board clock to
check the time.

I had sat almost an hour when I finally saw Jonathan walk toward his porch stairs wearing his sweats. That was my cue. I
waited until he entered the apartment, then I jumped out of my
car quickly, ran up the front steps, and pressed the rectangular, lit
doorbell. Did it work? I couldn't remember.

"Becky!"

"Hi, Jonathan. I came to visit you," I said as Jonathan opened
the door and I walked in.

We walked up the stairs, talking as friends.

"I just returned from an aerobics class," Jonathan said. "I'm having problems with my back and decided it was related to jogging.
Since I stopped jogging, the pain has gone away. So now I'm doing aerobics."

"I've stopped jogging too," I said, "due to knee problems. Remember when we first moved here and I jogged for five miles along
the beach with my old shoes instead of my new shoes, and injured
my knees?" He was having a difficult time remembering. Rightly so,
I suppose. That was a difficult time in our lives to recall. Our marriage was almost over then. "Remember, I couldn't walk without
pain for about a month afterwards?" I could see he still didn't recall.

"Maybe."

I followed Jonathan into the kitchen. He didn't ask to take my
coat, so I kept it on. I tried to make it seem that there was some
urgent reason for my visit. "Did you receive the package I sent
you?" I asked.

"No," Jonathan answered. "What package?"

"I found some things I thought you'd want. I'm sorry you didn't
receive the package I sent. It had some valuable things in it, like a

lock of hair your mother saved from when you were a baby, some *Christian Scholar* articles mentioning you, and your college ID's. Oh, I hope all that stuff was not lost. Let me know if you don't receive it, and I'll send a tracer."

Then I changed the subject. "I brought you some more things. Did I tell you about the person I met playing music in Concord who knew Granddad Lillis and is from Hinton, West Virginia? Can you believe his brother was the minister of Aunt Ruby's church? Small world!"

"That's unbelievable," Jonathan responded.

"Well," I said, "he brought in a book about Summers County, West Virginia." I pulled the xeroxed copy of the article from a folder and then asked Jonathan, "Do you know anyone in this picture?"

Jonathan recognized Aunt Ruby, but I had to point out my cousins and my grandmother. Jonathan recognized Granddad.

"Do you have some tea?" I asked.

"Yes," Jonathan answered in a tone of disbelief, indicating he thought it was incredible for me to be so bold.

I pulled off my coat and put it on the back of the kitchen chair and sat down. I looked around the kitchen. It was very clean and looked better than I remembered. The whole side of one wall had a variegated brick façade that looked almost pink. Against that wall sat the gas range and dishwasher that were now his. The wall adjacent was papered with a peach, gold, green, and brown pastel plaid that didn't exactly go with the brick, but it created a homey room. Against that wall was the refrigerator. On the next wall was a gold counter that went along most of the wall. It was odd that the cabinet construction had left a hole in the counter for the heat vent on the floor, which stood out like a missing tooth. It was clear the whole kitchen had been remodeled by a "do-it-yourselfer."

I sat on one of the chairs I had bought from a used furniture store in Ohio while visiting my sister one summer. It was part of an oak set and had been covered with several coats of green paint. Jonathan and I had both stripped and sanded down the table and chairs, then varnished them.

"Your kitchen looks nice and clean," I remarked.

"Well, don't look too closely," Jonathan said with a smile. "I don't do as well as you did. It really is a lot of work," he added as though to imply he hadn't appreciated how much work I did for him until having to do it himself. That made me feel good.

The tea kettle whistled, and I tried to find a mug. It was odd that I felt disoriented in what used to be my own kitchen. As I looked in the cupboards for a mug, I saw dishes that had been a wedding present from my parents.

"What are you looking for?" Jonathan asked.

"Mugs," I replied.

"They're on the wall."

Of course! I looked up at the mugs that also used to be mine. Some had been presents, and some were part of a set I had in my kitchen. I made my tea, and Jonathan prepared dinner.

"Do you want some soup?" Jonathan asked.

"Okay."

Jonathan poured me some clam chowder, made me a tuna sandwich, cut it in half, and put it on a plate. Then he sat down at the table. He said a nice prayer that thanked God for our food. It seemed natural to be eating dinner together again, and at the same time very odd. Tonight we were doing some of the same things we had done as a married couple, only now we were divorced.

"Your sandwich tastes good," I said. "It always tastes better when someone else makes it."

"Thanks."

Then I got down to brass tacks. "You know, there are many questions about our divorce and separation that I've never had the chance to ask. For instance, why did you show so little concern during the separation and divorce? When I wrote, you didn't call or respond."

Jonathan looked blankly at me and then said, "Remember what I did at the courthouse?"

"You mean when you hugged me?" I asked. "But that just made me mad. It made absolutely no sense to me. Why did you divorce me and then hug me? We shouldn't have gotten a divorce. There was much more good than bad in our marriage."

Jonathan just looked at me. There were no emotions surfacing. He had them completely under control.

"Why didn't you try to understand what had happened between us?" I asked. "Why didn't you try to see what went wrong?" Still there was no answer. "Why didn't you answer my letters, and why didn't you respond to my calls? It seems like you only wanted to avoid me. That's why I came unannounced, because I thought if you knew I was coming, you'd make an excuse not to see me."

"Why did you think that?" Jonathan asked.

"Well," I said, "let's take the last time I called you, for example. You acted as though you didn't want to talk at all. You told me that you had to go because your lunch was on the stove. You cut the conversation short."

"What did you want me to do?" Jonathan asked. "My lunch was going to burn!"

"You could have said, 'Can you please wait a moment while I turn the stove off? My lunch is going to burn.' If you called me and the situation was reversed, what would you have thought?"

I started to feel frustrated. He didn't understand my message. I had to tell myself to be patient. At that moment it became very clear to me why our marriage had failed—communication problems! Jonathan received a different message from the one I sent. We both were misunderstood.

I continued, "And why did you send those letters to my family? The letter to my mother and Tanya? Why?" Jonathan started to look uncomfortable, like a child accused of something he had not done.

"I miss them," Jonathan said simply. "Was it wrong for me to send them letters?"

I started in again. "You know why you sent them? Because you still love me, and I still love you!" I looked him straight in the eyes. "Remember last year when you came to my house to make the divorce settlement? Do you remember what I told you? It was right before you left. I said to you, 'You know, I'll never find another person as good as you.'" I was trying to work up the courage to add another phrase. I started again, "I'll never find anyone as good as you," and then I quickly added, "and you won't find anyone as good as me either! We paid dearly for all we've learned from this divorce and separation, and I don't want to use what I've learned in this marriage on someone else. I want to know if you'd be interested in trying to restore the relationship. We need each other. I am the emotional side of you, and you are the logical side of me."

Jonathan looked uncomfortable. I couldn't believe myself. What was I saying? Did I really want to go back with him? Was I caught up in the excitement of the moment without realizing what I was saying? Was I willing to follow through if he should take me up on my offer? I didn't know the answer, but I could see that Jonathan was listening to me. I felt that this was a very tentative situation and that I could only proceed with extreme caution. I didn't want to overwhelm Jonathan or confuse him. Most of all, I didn't want to scare him into retreat. I didn't feel that Jonathan was horrified by what I was saying. I believed he was open and receptive. I looked at the clock. It was a little past eight. We had been together for an hour.

"I have a long drive back," I said. "I'd better leave. I have to get up early for work." We both left the table.

"Maybe we could get together once a week and start seeing each other again."

"Once a week!" Jonathan exclaimed. "That's a bit much for me!"

"Once a month?"

There was no answer.

"Well, think about what I've said."

"I'll think about it," Jonathan said.

Then we walked toward the stairway leading outside. We hugged each other. It felt so good to hug Jonathan. His sweatshirt felt soft, and I felt at home. Jonathan walked me outside, and I got into my car. As I turned it around in the driveway across the street I rolled down the window, and as I drove by I tooted the horn and waved. I could see him as he stood alone watching me as I drove away into the night.

•

"Hi, Jonathan. This is Becky."

"I know who it is. I suppose you're calling to ask about my reaction to your visit."

"Yes," I answered, "I thought maybe it would be good if we could get together and talk about what has happened to us over the last two years. How do you feel about that?"

"Well," he said cautiously, "I may agree to talk about it." Then I heard the unspoken implication, "but that's all—I don't want to get back together."

"I was wondering if you would like to come out Friday?" I asked. "There is a contra dance at my church. It's good for beginners, and it's lot of fun. You could stay over and sleep on my air mattress, and then the next day we could walk in the woods behind my cottage."

"I'll give it some thought," Jonathan replied.

"Okay."

It seemed like there was nothing more to say. It was as though we had nothing in common at all and had never known each other before. We had only exchanged words. There was a stilted silence; neither Jonathan nor I volunteered the next word, so I concluded the conversation.

"You can think it over and let me know. You have plenty of time."

"Okay."

"It was nice talking with you," I said. "Goodbye."

I tried to have faith. The fact that Jonathan and I had agreed to meet and discuss our divorce seemed like a positive sign, but I was reading too much into the situation, and I wasn't taking Jonathan literally the way he was supposed to be taken. Instead I was trying to interpret events, emotions, and signs, and guess what Jonathan was saying. Did I know Jonathan better than he knew himself? No. I just wanted to believe in our love, and I wanted to believe we would reconcile. I even took Jonathan's picture out of my dresser drawer and set it on top of the dresser as a testimony of my faith.

But it was a last-ditch effort to put things back as they had been and to recover what was lost. It was a desperate attempt to apply the Christian "born-again" ethic to my marital crisis. The church taught that divorce was against the "will of God" and that it was a dishonor. So if I wanted what God wanted, couldn't I tap into God's power to help save our relationship? Before I hadn't known that poor communication was the main cause of our difficulties. But now I did, so couldn't I take steps now to correct the problem? Or had too much time gone by? Did either of us care enough to start all over with the relationship and try again?

Ten Months After Divorce

Two weeks passed before I decided to call Jonathan at work and ask him again when we could schedule our talk.

"Hello, Jonathan. I am calling to find out if you are coming on Friday to visit."

"Two weeks have passed? I thought you invited me in three weeks."

"No."

"I don't remember that I agreed to meet with you," Jonathan said.

"I thought you agreed to talk about the divorce," I replied.

"Well, I'm having company that weekend. Byron Delbene [a college friend] is coming with his two boys."

"Can we reschedule it for another time? How about the following weekend? I can come to Plymouth on Friday and then stay over with Nigel and Christine. We could go out to eat and then talk."

"That wouldn't be a good time. I'll be extremely busy that week. What about during spring vacation?"

"I'm planning to visit my family then," I said.

"How about next Monday night?" Jonathan asked.

"No. Mondays are usually too busy for me." I replied. "It looks like we'll never get a time when we're both free. Let's try a get-together during the middle of the day." It seemed like pulling teeth would be easier than getting to meet with Jonathan.

"How would next Thursday be during the noon hour for lunch?" I asked.

"All right," Jonathan said.

"I'll give you my phone number at work," I said. "Once you get to the main information desk at the hospital, you can use the house phone and call me when you arrive."

"Okay. Is there a place to eat?" Jonathan asked.

"Yes," I replied. "We have four cafeterias."

"Okay. I'll see you next Thursday."

I had finally gotten him committed to a day to meet with me. Then I thought for a moment. What a place and time to talk about the last two years of our lives and their significance—a cafeteria where there was no privacy, and with the time limit of one hour! After sleeping on it, I decided to change the meeting time and place. I called him at work the next day.

"Hi, Jonathan." Jonathan didn't seem overly surprised by my call, but he didn't sound pleased either. "I'm calling because I'd like to change our meeting to a place that is more private and to a time where we won't be rushed."

"Why?" Jonathan asked.

I told myself to be patient, and I tried to explain to him the downfalls of meeting me in the cafeteria at work. "Do you think a cafeteria is a private place?" I asked.

"I haven't seen your cafeteria."

"But a cafeteria is a cafeteria, isn't it? They aren't usually quiet and private. Do you think a cafeteria is an appropriate place to talk about something as complex as our divorce?" I asked. "Can't you see that a more appropriate place for such a discussion would be in a quiet, private setting?"

Reluctantly Jonathan said, "I guess I can see your point. Where would you rather have this discussion?"

"How about in your apartment or mine? I called Christine yesterday and she said I could stay over at her house for the night, so we could meet in a restaurant, have dinner, then go to your apartment and talk. I could stay with Nigel and Christine for the night." Jonathan didn't seem very excited about that prospect, and he didn't volunteer any other time to get together. "When could we schedule our talk?" I tried again. At least now Jonathan did accept the fact that he had agreed to have a talk with me.

"Now is a really bad time for me at school," Jonathan answered. "I have so many meetings for different committees; it's a really bad time to schedule anything. I'll have to get back to you for a time. I don't have my calendar with me."

"Okay, that's fine," I said feeling a bit impatient.

"So our meeting for Thursday in the cafeteria is off, then?" Jonathan asked almost in a tone of relief.

"Yes," I said. "The point is to schedule a more appropriate place and time where we can talk privately without being rushed. That's why we're not meeting in the cafeteria next week."

Several days went by. I expected he'd find a time he could see me, then call back, but I didn't hear from him.

It was a Sunday afternoon when I called Jonathan again. I had just gone for a walk in the beautiful woods behind my house and had missed companionship, someone with whom to share the beauty. In the past Jonathan and I had enjoyed many walks in the woods together, and I longed for him to be with me today. At that moment my feelings for him were strong so I called him.

"Hi, Jonathan. Did you come up with a date we can get together?" I asked. I felt like a pesky sales person trying to wear down the client.

"Well, how about April sixth?" Jonathan asked. "That will be the last day of classes."

"Okay, that's good for me too. I was planning to visit home, but I've decided to wait and visit my family at the end of the month." It seemed strange to say "my family" as though I were talking to a stranger. Not only did Jonathan know my family well, but they used to be his family too.

"Why don't you come to my place?" I asked. "I've been to yours twice already."

"Okay."

"And you can come for dinner, too." (Maybe I was getting a bit carried away). "And if you want to stay over, I have an extra bed. The next day we could go hiking in the woods."

"I'd like to see your church," Jonathan said.

"I'm sure you would," I replied. "You know, the bell in the steeple was cast by Paul Revere. By the way, I'm joining the church in several days. I love everything about this beautiful, old, colonial New England church."

"That's great, Becky!"

Perhaps I thought that if Jonathan knew I was joining a church, he'd see that I was a good person after all. I was surprised by his increased participation in the conversation, so I continued to talk.

"You can ask me any questions you want when you come."

"I don't know that I'll ask you any questions," Jonathan said.

"And it will be a friendly exchange about what has happened to us both during these last two years."

"Okay."

"All right," I said. "So I'll see you April sixth."

Eleven Months After Divorce

On the evening of April 6 I wore a new dress, and my table was set with china and red carnations. At around 7:00 p.m. there was a knock at the door; it was Jonathan.

"I had forgotten how far out here you live."

"How long did it take you to get here?"

"About an hour and fifteen minutes."

As soon as Jonathan entered my kitchen he looked with interest at my big green refrigerator, which was covered with pictures of my family. Some were baby pictures of my nieces and nephews—several born after our separation and divorce.

"Who's that?" Jonathan asked.

"Jennifer's [my sister] new baby, Anita. Those are all of Anita," I said as I pointed out several pictures of her that had been sent to me by my sister.

Jonathan told me proudly that Tanya had sent him Bryan's birth announcement. I had heard that news before, one visit ago. It must have made him feel good that my family still cared enough to inform him of important events.

"And there's Steve [my brother]," Jonathan said.

Then I pointed to another picture and asked, "See the yellow wooden walls behind Steve? That's the inside of Mom and Dad's house—all yellow and warm—the color of new wood."

Then he gave me updates on his family. Most of the news I had heard during our last meeting two months ago, including a statement that one of my former sister-in-laws had taken my new address and said she wanted to stay in touch with me, which made me feel good.

Jonathan and I had an agreeable conversation as long as we didn't touch any emotional issues. The dinner seemed pleasant enough. I found it ironic that we were divorced but were sharing dinner again, as we had many times during our fifteen-year marriage. Yet this was different, for we were at my own place in the rural setting where I had chosen to live, rather than a location to accommodate his schooling or career. The conversation never came close to the real reason we were meeting. It began to look like we were purposely avoiding the topic, but then to my surprise Jonathan said, "Why don't we talk about us?"

That was a loaded question. If, for instance, a couple asked this question after seeing each other for several years, it could lead to a proposal of marriage. The question could mean, "Do you want to spend the rest of your life with me?" or it could mean, "I find our relationship stimulating and meaningful and I'd like to see if you feel the same." Even in this setting the question could have had more than one meaning. It could mean, "Let's talk about how we can rebuild our relationship," or "Let's talk about what happened to us these last two years." The more contact I had with Jonathan during this period, the more I learned not to read meaning into anything he said or did, as I found myself doing at that moment.

"Okay. I know the question I want to ask," I said. "What do you think happened? Why are we divorced?"

Jonathan pressed his lips together and looked very thoughtful for a moment and then began to speak in a very slow and deliberate fashion, putting in many pauses. "I think for various reasons, at the end, there was a lot of pent-up anger and resentment. I think you were angry because you were forced to go outside the relationship for happiness. I realize that things happened that you felt you couldn't tell me about. Somehow there was a major break-down in communication."

That was it! Communication! That's what I thought too! I was very surprised we had both come to the same conclusion. I thought he would link all of our problems to my spiritual back-sliding and "fall from church."

"What do you think happened?" he asked.

"I think we didn't speak each other's language. I came from a very emotional family, and you didn't. My family communicated with feelings more than words, and we read between the lines. Since you were from an unemotional family, you were taught to communicate in a different way. When we communicated, we sent each other messages that were never received because we couldn't understand each other's language. Since we didn't really know what the problem was, we didn't know how to fix it. Now things look more clear. Now I can think of ways to solve some of our past problems. Take for example the church conflicts. Now I'd suggest that we attend separate churches. It is easier to see solutions to our problems now that I'm away from the situation, looking back."

"Do you think that's why we got a divorce, because of the church?" Jonathan asked defensively.

"No," I responded. "I was just using that as an example. I think church was only part of the problem. It seems we are in agreement as to what the real problem was."

"Do you have any more questions?" Jonathan was feeling braver than me, as though this ordeal wasn't so bad after all.

"Why did you desert me when I needed you most?" I asked.

There was an interval of silence. He seemed surprised and asked, "Who left whom?"

"But, Jonathan, don't you remember I asked if I could come back? I asked you more than once. I asked you within three months of leaving and countless times afterwards, both before and after divorce. I was reaching out to you for help, love, and under-standing, and I received nothing in return."

It seemed that Jonathan had never thought of it that way

before, that I had been left instead of him. After a pained expression, Jonathan began to share with me the suffering I had caused him. "It hurt first of all when you left me; and then, as if that wasn't enough, your involvement with lovers during our marriage hurt me. Finally, your continued involvement after our separation literally broke my heart. I just couldn't believe it. After you told me of your last involvement, I felt as though I had been raped and that I was literally going to die. I thought my heart would stop beating. I felt my heart had been broken into a million pieces, never to be restored again. After that point, there was nothing to do but move forward into a new life."

"But if you only knew that I had been a victim," I said. "I was vulnerable and broken."

"I'm sorry if it seemed like I wasn't supportive or that I didn't care what was happening to you."

I felt very sad about the magnitude of pain I had caused Jonathan. If only he had been able to express that pain to me before we divorced or before he stopped loving me. His expression of pain affected me deeply. Why couldn't I have seen or felt this before? Because he couldn't express his feelings to me, it didn't mean he had no feelings. The way it had appeared to me was not actually the way it had been.

I wasn't sure if I should ask the next question. It would be difficult. "How was what you did with Sharon any different from what I did with Mark?" Jonathan looked at me in disbelief, as though I had gone insane. How could I even ask such a question? He prepared his defense and spoke deliberately and with conviction. "I had set up very strict rules and guidelines that I carefully adhered to."

It was too much for me. I broke in as my anger skyrocketed. "Oh, right! Just because you didn't have intercourse, you think that means you weren't unfaithful? What about emotional infidelity? You were still my husband until last August, you know. You were seeing another woman, and you were my husband!"

Rules, rules! If it weren't for rules in every facet of Jonathan's life, he would probably have disintegrated. As long as he had the security of his rules, he could feel right about his behavior, about his life, and about being emotionally unfaithful.

"If I hadn't talked to Sharon, I would have gone crazy."

"And if I didn't have Mark," I said, "who understood me and was sensitive to my music, I would have gone crazy."

He could not see the parallel, and he never would. Because I broke the big rule, "Thou shalt not commit adultery," we were worlds apart, although the shadows of gray that defined adultery were not even considered. Jonathan found comfort in his rules and freedom from guilt concerning his behavior. I thought there was a very fine line separating the difference between our situations, but Jonathan felt our behavior was separated by a chasm.

"I...I am going to leave shortly," Jonathan said as he glanced nervously at his watch.

I looked down at my dessert plate, the brownie that was wading in a small pool of melted chocolate chip ice cream. My appetite for it vanished as I moved the brownie chunk along the ice cream river with my spoon.

"Let's move into the living room," I said in an effort to change the tense tone. I put our dishes into the small stainless steel sink and covered them with water.

When we walked into the living room, Jonathan looked shocked at seeing the Victorian furniture that had belonged to my mom and dad. It was a reminder of our past and the good family memories of spending holidays together. Was my furniture causing Jonathan the same kind of pain that last year's items Jonathan had brought from my past had caused me?

"How did they get here?" Jonathan asked almost in shock.

"I carried them in my hatchback."

Jonathan still stared at the chairs as though he'd seen a ghost. "But how did you get them here?" He asked again as though he had not heard my answer.

"Both these chairs, the table, and the lamp fit in my car."

He walked over to one of the beautiful gold velvet chairs, the captain's chair, and sat down, almost in a trance. I sat on the sofa at one end, alone with all the pillows surrounding me. I seemed to feel the presence of another person—a woman to whom Jonathan was now remaining true. He would not want to spark her jealousy in any way, and so he behaved as though she were with him. Jonathan was now following Sharon's rules.

"I have just a couple more questions. I wrote them down on a card because I didn't want to forget them," I said as I reached into a manila folder to pull out the card. I had prepared for this visit like an interview.

"Okay."

"One thing really bothers me. Do you think I didn't love you when we were married?"

"No. I think you loved me."

"Good. I don't want you to think I didn't love you, because as hard as it may be for you to understand, I really did." Then it struck me, I hadn't used the present tense. I had said "did" not "do." Had I really fallen out of love with my ex-husband, or was I afraid of saying "love" because he no longer had love for me?"

"How do you interpret my unfaithfulness?" I asked.

"I think you were unhappy and frustrated."

"Good," I said. "I didn't want you to think it happened because I didn't love you. Those are all the questions I have. The main one was, 'What do you think happened?' I'm glad we've both come to the same conclusion about the communication."

"Do you think we could ever correct that problem?" Jonathan asked.

"I don't think it would be impossible. Here's where I believe counseling might help. We would both have to learn each other's language. I think we'd have to want to do it more than anything in the world. It would be very difficult." Did that mean Jonathan wanted to try? What if he did? Would I want to try too?

"How do you feel about me now, Jonathan?" I wanted to know if he still loved me.

He hesitated and carefully selected his words. "I'll always care about you, Becky. I want you to be happy."

"That's nice, Jonathan. I'll always care about you, too." Jonathan didn't say he loved me, and although I had felt strong love for him a month earlier, I couldn't say I loved him this day.

"Those are all the questions I have for you. Have you any for me?"

"No."

"Well, then, I have something I'd like you to read." I walked into the bedroom and pulled out a manila folder containing hundreds of pages all about my divorce. "This is how I got through my divorce, by writing my journal."

A year ago I had wanted to try to reach Jonathan—to communicate with him through my written words. My writing was a desperate attempt to reach out to him so he would understand the emotions I had felt during our separation and divorce. I had thought that if I could explain my side clearly and completely, he would understand and then want to reconcile our marriage. But tonight I only wanted him to gain a deeper knowledge of what had happened between us so that there could be a more satisfying resolution or closure. Since all my attempts at conveying my story to him verbally had failed miserably, I wondered if my journal writing had been meant for this night.

I handed my journal to Jonathan. I had chosen two passages for him to read. The first one was about our mutual friend Barbara Hachett, and showed an effort to have all my religious friends pray for a miracle to happen between Jonathan and me. When Jonathan read the entry that said I was a "sinner," he seemed a little touched.

"You felt that way?" he asked. Perhaps he now knew I felt regret for my unfaithfulness.

Then I thought it best to share my journal entry for the day we were both together—the day in divorce court. Jonathan read the whole thing aloud to me as I lay on the couch and listened. The passage brought back all the painful memories of that day, some of which I had not thought about for quite some time. What did Jonathan think? Was I reaching him? Did he understand my message?

Because of Jonathan's quiet way, I could not read his emotions. I could not tell whether he was pleased, hurt, amazed, unhappy, or touched. There was no evidence of any emotional reaction, which was interpreted by me (probably incorrectly) as indifference. I had no idea whether my attempt to help Jonathan understand my side of the divorce had succeeded or failed.

"You mean you went to work after that?" Jonathan had just learned that I had gone back to work after our session in divorce court.

"Yes. My boss was out of town, so I had his office to myself. I didn't accomplish much, but I went to work," I said. "I mostly laid on my boss's couch and cried."

He seemed amazed. I wondered why, but didn't ask.

Soon it looked as though Jonathan had had enough for one evening. He glanced at the digital clock on the stereo he had given me and acted as though he had to leave quickly in order to be on time for another appointment. He had been at my house two and a half hours. I didn't understand the urgency of his quick departure, for the next day started spring break; but I could see that he wanted to leave, and to my surprise I was ready for him to go.

I looked at this man who used to be my husband. His outward appearance was the same, but he was different inside. He was more withdrawn and even more cautious than before. Perhaps the pain I had caused him had pushed him back even further into his shell, so that he would never know the wonderful joy of freely expressing and communicating emotions.

As we walked toward the kitchen door, I was surprised that I did not want the moments to last longer so that I could treasure them. I realized that I no longer felt love for Jonathan. I cared deeply for him, but felt no love. I looked at him as though I had never seen him before, and I felt no attraction. He was a nice person, but I did not want a relationship with him. It was as though all the common bonds we had shared for fifteen years had been broken or had never existed at all. I stood a distance from him as we said goodbye, then watched as he walked out the door toward his car. Could it be that I no longer wanted a reconciliation with Jonathan? Was I finally learning to let go and move forward with my life? As he drove away I felt pleased at what had transpired that evening. I felt good about myself and surprised that I was not crying or feeling regret over leaving Jonathan. Our closure talk had been beneficial for me and, I hoped, for Jonathan too.

At least at that hour, I felt no desire to return to my former life. There had been a temporary lull in the pain, which gave me enough encouragement to want to believe I was over my divorce. But I wasn't; I had not even been divorced two years. There was still a long road ahead full of regret, guilt, unhappiness, and loneliness. But the small oasis of relief I felt that night was a welcome reprieve, and I embraced it.

11. Looking Back

I wasn't even halfway through my divorce when my journal ended. Although most of the sleepless nights were over, pain, regret, loneliness, and guilt remained for nearly six years. During discouraging times I looked unrealistically at my former married life and wished it had never ended. When I measured my present life next to a romanticized past, it always fell short. By leaving Jonathan I believed I had made a mistake that I would regret the rest of my life.

When I had been the one to leave, why had I fantasized of reuniting with my ex-husband? The timing was a factor. At the beginning of our separation, I was full of anger that had been repressed during our marriage. The anger had helped motivate me to leave my husband during a time when my love for him was present, albeit numb. But eight months later the novelty of my separation had grown old, and I had encountered difficulties in finding compatible companions, so I began to believe Jonathan was superior to anyone I could possibly meet in the future. Then it made sense to me that we work on our relationship rather than start anew with different partners. As I faced hardship and loneliness, I romanticized my past life with my husband. I forgot about the strict religious rules that had restricted my life-style, and I forgot about my unfulfilling sex life with my husband—all the marital problems I had left behind. The absence of Jonathan's love in my life seemed to devalue that which I had considered most important when we were married: my music, being close to nature, freedom to choose my own place of worship and religious philosophy. What I took for granted when married, I appreciated when separated. Likewise, the good life I had gained through my separation and divorce I took for granted, for I then could only recall the good from my marriage—none of the bad. Longing to reunite with my husband was a romanticized fantasy that only stopped haunting me once I had reached divorce recovery.

Before my recovery I was haunted not only by memories of my ex-husband, but also by an overwhelming burden of guilt that remained with me because I felt responsible for the break-up of my marriage. I had wanted one more chance at reconciliation, but it had been denied because I had told Jonathan about a new affair two months after our separation. This broke Jonathan's heart so completely that all he could do was divorce me. This rejection by Jonathan reaffirmed my guilt and confirmed to me that I was the one at fault.

A bad self-image resulted, and my confidence plummeted. Every day at work I was reminded of my poor career decision to leave sales and become a medical secretary again. In addition, due to my new start-up expenses, it became financially difficult. I applied for credit cards several times and was turned down; it was humiliating and discouraging. The fact that I was not able to provide a better standard of living for myself reinforced my poor self-esteem.

I wanted to begin anew and thought that moving to be near my family would help comfort me during my recovery. In addition, since I believed I could never afford my own home, the lure of a rent-free place on six acres owned by my father convinced me to move out of state. However, this proved to be a bitter disappointment and a financial drain because I could not find suitable permanent employment. My standard of living dropped even lower, and the artistic and cultural stimulation I required were almost non-existent. A year later I returned to Boston to my former medical secretarial job (my replacement had left).

My personal life had also been discouraging. During my first two years of separation and divorce, after involvement with eight different men (four of whom were married), I began to realize that single or divorced men compatible with me were difficult to find. Many single men were single for a good reason. They either weren't capable of handling a close, committed relationship or they were too selfish to love someone other than themselves.

It was during the first half of my divorce recovery, when my esteem was very low, that I became involved with a married man who became a part-time lover for two years. At the beginning, during the infatuation stage, the relationship lifted my spirits; it gave a much-needed boost to my ego and temporarily made me feel loved. But it eventually degenerated into a relationship of convenient sex, and at the end it only made me feel worse about myself.

During half of the time I was involved with my married lover, I also had a single lover, although both men together did not equal one relationship. My single lover was from my past and was fond of me, but this relationship also degenerated into convenient sex. He determined when we'd be together, and it was usually arranged to include one of my home-cooked meals. For me, this part-time relationship was similar to being involved with a married man, except that he was married to his career and his personal life of nursing his elderly parents. Although I was experiencing fulfilling sex from a physical standpoint, I began to wonder if I would ever again have someone to love me. No one since my husband had.

It all caved in on me when I reached my fortieth birthday and began to take inventory of my life. At that point I felt I had few achievements of which to feel proud. But what distressed me most was that I had no lover who really loved me. It was then that my need for intimacy and love became overpowering. I felt that without intimacy and love to nourish my spirit, my life was worthless. Then it became overwhelmingly clear that I urgently had to find an intimate love.

Three years after divorce, I joined a dating club for singles who were classical musicians. Seven months later, after thirteen blind dates, I became discouraged, then decided to place a personal ad with a different service. However, since my membership with the classical music club had not expired, I began to use it solely to find musicians to fill vacancies in my chamber music groups. I needed a keyboard player and contacted three. One wasn't advanced enough, the second never returned my call, and the third was named Mario.

Mario, a romantic, handsome Italian pianist who preferred Rachmaninov, Chopin, and Brahms to early composers, was not convinced he would enjoy playing Telemann on the harpsichord with my group. But I persuaded him to join us for a trial rehearsal, and he, being open-minded, agreed. Upon our first meeting, we had instant chemistry. Our second date initiated a whirlwind romance that we both believed would end in two months, but our needs and interests were the same, and our timing was perfectly coordinated. When Mario said he loved me I was overjoyed, for I loved him too. Mario had the capacity to love and express it to me in a way I could understand, which resulted in a wonderful, intimate relationship that became the most important and loving one of my life.

When I first met Mario I still had not recovered entirely from my divorce. I had lost faith in myself and believed I was a dysfunctional person who could never remain faithful to one lover. Very early in my relationship with Mario, I honestly told him about my unfaithfulness to Jonathan. I wanted to warn him about me before we became too involved. I also told him of my recent involvement with two lovers, and I painted for him a bleak picture because I doubted myself. But Mario believed in me and gave me the chance I desperately needed to prove to myself that I was strong, whole, and good.

One by one, former lovers with whom I had been involved while married called or came to Boston on business. When they contacted me it was clear they hoped to mix business with sexual pleasure, but each time my response was the same. I told them of Mario and our love, then rejected their propositions. I rejoiced inwardly because each time I did this, I was rewriting my personal history. I was proving that I was in fact a strong, healthy person in control of my life, who knew what I wanted and how to achieve it!

During that year I regained my integrity. Mario's healing, nurturing love had helped me to believe again in myself.

Another factor, the passing of time, also helped me recover from divorce. It took five years to reach recovery. Like the aging of fine wine, the process could not be rushed. Although I tried to help my recovery by reading self-help books and talking with friends and relatives, the lessons I needed to learn could only come through experience. Experience took time, and time brought healing.

My writing was also important in my recovery from divorce. It gave me an outlet through which my pain and confusion could be expressed. Not only was it a medium through which I could vent my feelings, it helped me uncover the answers to questions that had troubled me for years, even during my marriage. I had forgotten about the abnormal sex life between Jonathan and me early in our marriage. In my guilt, I had only focused on the fact that I had been unfaithful, which made me feel I was the one mostly at fault for our divorce. Only through my writing and research did I come to see that there were reasons why I had committed adultery. I had wanted to believe all along in their existence, but I hadn't been able to point to evidence in my favor until I uncovered it in diaries from early in my marriage. This unlocked the door to understanding why I had been unfaithful, which arrested my guilt and promoted my healing.

In addition, there were two other events that also helped in my recovery. The first was a scheduled meeting with Jonathan. Four years after divorce, I put together a photo album from a collection of pictures I had taken of Jonathan and his family throughout our fifteen-year marriage. I wanted to present them in person, for I wanted to see him again. By this time Jonathan had remarried, so I knew my visit would not be threatening. I contacted Jonathan, and he agreed to meet me at his Christian college office.

The experience was overwhelming. It was as though I had journeyed back in time. Years ago, during the summer months when school was out, the outside door to his building was often locked. It was locked the day I visited Jonathan again. I did the same thing

I had done in this situation years before—I threw a rock lightly at his window to get his attention. The rock produced the same effect this time as it did before: Jonathan came to the door to let me in. We exchanged our greetings, then walked together to his third-floor office. There I handed him the photo album—perhaps a symbolic peace offering. We looked at it together, and I pointed out the photos of him that I especially liked. Then he showed me his doctoral thesis, which acknowledged my help.

Then, with tears streaming down my face, I apologized to Jonathan for having hurt him. I cried for a multitude of reasons. That day Jonathan seemed like the old Jonathan I remembered from the good times of our marriage. My tears were mourning the good in our former relationship that could never be recovered. But I also cried for the hope of both our futures—separately.

Soon it was time for our visit to end. I reached to shake his hand, but to my surprise he hugged me instead. It was a very touching moment. Then he walked me to my car and stood there waving until I drove out of sight. For an hour I had turned back the clock's hands; it almost felt like we were once again husband and wife. The tension between us was gone—time had healed the strife that divorce had put between us. At that moment I could no longer remember what had been wrong with our relationship and why we had separated and divorced. My brief visit with Jonathan had been good, and it had affected me deeply. The next day I couldn't control my tears. When friends at work asked me why I was crying, I could not speak. My crying was an impulsive reaction that only lasted a day. I was crying tears of closure for the final chapter of my divorce.

The second event that helped my recovery was buying my own home. During my marriage, due to my lack of self-confidence, I had often used Jonathan's strengths to compensate for my weaknesses. I had felt my intelligence was only average in comparison to Jonathan's brilliance and that I was too emotional in comparison to Jonathan's logical personality; he was all I would never be. When we separated, I had doubts I could even survive on my own without his help. However, all my self-doubts were put to rest when I closed escrow on a three-bedroom house after securing a special first-time mortgage through an agency targeting low-middle-income buyers. I did this all alone—on my own, with no help from anyone. The fact that I had achieved this lifelong goal with my own strength, without Jonathan's help, convinced me that I could do anything. Buying a house on my own income was nothing short of a miracle! I began to believe again in my abilities, my reasoning, and my intuition. I had proven to myself that I could make good decisions on my own. With the evidence plainly before me and the keys to my house in my hand, I could no longer have the faintest doubt that I was capable of providing for myself. In fact, I had drastically improved what had been my standard of living when I was Jonathan's wife. My new life in my new house convinced me that there was no reason to hold on to my past. My present life was best.

Within six months of moving into my house, I came upon a list of my needs, made during my counseling sessions. I had never given much thought to my needs before counseling. It was not something my former religion encouraged. We had been taught, "God shall supply all your need according to his riches in glory by Christ Jesus." (Philippians 4:19) It was a category we let God handle exclusively. However, even if I could have focused on my needs during marriage, they would have been modified for Jonathan. He came first. He was the head of the family and I was his helpmate, so it was my duty to help him reach his goals regardless of my needs. My counselor asked me repeatedly to list my needs, because she could tell I didn't know what they were. After my separation from Jonathan, I made the following list: 1. Country living; 2. Own place (rent or own); 3. Pleasing environment (aesthetics); 4. Freedom to practice, study, and rehearse music; 5. Control over paycheck; 6. Time alone; 7. Freedom from Jonathan's church; 8. Good or great sex; 9. Excitement; 10. Love; 11. Outdoor activity; 12. Being understood (same communication medium); 13. Sharing music with someone I love; 14. Working in agreeable environments in the arts; 15. Performing music; 16. Romance; 17. Flexibility (e.g., time off). At that time fourteen out of seventeen needs were being met. The list remained lost in a notebook until I moved into my new home, when it was found. Much to my surprise, within eight years, all of the needs on my list had been met but one: number 14. And I was still working on it! Although I had not seen the list in years, my needs had been internalized, and subconsciously I had been working toward meeting them.

In looking back now, I believe this was my key to recovery. Identifying my needs was basic—the first step. It was the beginning of reconstructing my devastated life again from square one. Each time a need was met, it freed up more of my energy to apply to another area of my life. Once my most urgent needs of companionship and intimacy were met, I had the energy necessary to concentrate on a creative way to buy a house. Once that need was met, I had the energy to explore an area in my life that I had always had an interest in—my writing. Each need that was met increased my confidence, my strength, and my happiness.

Recovery came for me five years after my divorce. I don't know the day it occurred, for the realization took place only after I had passed that point and looked back. It was gradual in coming and was noticed only when I recognized that I no longer wished I were still married to Jonathan. When I no longer asked myself if my present was better than my past, I was over my divorce. Eventually it became overwhelmingly obvious that my new life was most wonderful and was the best of all I had experienced. It could be compared to the arrival of spring, which came very gradually after a harsh winter. The new buds were unnoticed until the leaves were fully out and green. The blossoms were suddenly in full bloom with all their fragrance. It was then that my heart was filled with gladness as a sense of renewal and hope swept me into a new era of contentment and joy.

As I look back upon my marriage after being single for eight years, I see more clearly what I was desperately trying to understand those first two years of separation and divorce—what went wrong. Now I know that my nourishment comes from intimacy, and after spending fifteen years in a relationship where there was none, I see why it was necessary to leave. I was starving for love I could feel and for communication that resulted in understanding. For without being understood it was impossible to be known, and without being known, there would never be intimacy.

Not only did I need emotional intimacy, I needed physical intimacy as well. My diary from the first year of my marriage clearly showed that my marriage had a very abnormal beginning physically. So I buried my sexual drive and tried to concentrate on the positive aspects of my marriage. Although repression worked for seven years, eventually the pain and disappointment resulting from my unfulfilled needs sprang forth as a sexual obsession. The outlet through which I eventually found physical gratification was my affairs.

There were other factors in our divorce. We married at the early ages of twenty-one and twenty-two, when our personalities had not completely developed. We both changed in fifteen years, and these changes brought friction. Jonathan grew more conservative, and I grew more liberal. It was ironic that our common background in the Wesleyan denomination, which had brought us together at a church-supported college, eventually became a source of contention between us. As I matured and began to form my own theological beliefs, I went from embracing this church to rejecting it. But Jonathan's devotion to this Christian church only increased, for it not only ordered his life but defined who he was. As I began to reject the church, it seemed to Jonathan that I rejected him.

By choosing my own religious beliefs, it would be impossible for Jonathan and I to co-exist peaceably, for his way only was acceptable in our family unit. As I pulled away from Jonathan's church and enjoyed socializing more with musicians and people outside the church family, Jonathan increased his church activities. When I pointed out to Jonathan the church's inconsistencies, I was seen as "bad-mouthing" the church and its people. My attempts to show Jonathan my beliefs were useless, for to him, the church environment meant survival. To me it meant death. For my own personal growth, I needed to be free. How sad that this church, which promoted God's love, became a wedge between two whose union had been blessed by the very same church.

This evangelical Christian denomination not only affected my relationship with Jonathan during our marriage, but long before we ever met it influenced our adult behavior. I believe it was partially responsible for our unfulfilling sex during the early years of our marriage. I can recall as a teenager hearing sermons that denounced the "ways of the flesh." "But I say unto you that whosoever looketh on a woman to lust after her hath committed adultery with her already in his heart. And if thy right eye offend thee, cut it off, and cast it from thee: for it is profitable for thee that one of thy members should perish and not that thy whole body should be cast into hell." (Matthew 5:28-29) Since Jonathan was a sincere believer, he most likely resisted these unclean urges and thoughts until he became almost asexual. Once our marriage had sanctioned intercourse, Jonathan had to learn to become comfortable with his sexuality—a process that took him nearly seven years. By this time I was so discouraged with our sex life that I was already emotionally out of the marriage, and physically as well.

Our church background even affected the way in which Jonathan and I tried to solve our physical problems. My diary from the first year of our marriage documents that I took the issue to the Lord in prayer and trusted that He would provide a solution. I waited and trusted God. Four years later, after the problem had worsened, Jonathan and I attended a New Life Seminar held by a Christian couple who gave seminars designed to improve marriages. They promoted the belief that the answers to all of life's problems were contained in the Bible. So I then applied their cure of Bible study, prayer, and scripture memorization to my physical relationship with Jonathan. This remedy did not work.

Probably the most damaging attitude that Jonathan and I inherited from our church background was the lack of self-knowledge and assertiveness. Both are related, because they involve one's will. Self-knowledge means knowing enough about one's self that one can define one's needs. Assertiveness means having the courage and capability and energy to fulfill those needs. By having both self-knowledge and assertiveness, one's will is strengthened, and one knows who one is and where one is going.

I can recall hearing many sermons in our church about doing God's will. This is because we were taught that man was bent toward sin. So following my will would lead to an unfulfilling life of hopelessness. The alternative was to do God's will instead of my own, because He always knows what is best for our lives. In following God's will I would be certain to find His plan for my life, happiness, and God's blessings.

In the process of extinguishing our will and seeking God's, our self-knowledge becomes muddled and buried. Instead of developing a healthy assertiveness and self-love to help us survive in this world and take care of ourselves, we instead learn to wait (for God) while being unassertive or indecisive. The church's way teaches us to remain open to God's will and not to follow our own will.

Another factor that contributed to our marital difficulties was deadlock. This psychological state occurs when the dynamics of the relationship are frozen—when both parties are trapped in unequal and opposing roles all of the time. I was in the submissive role, and Jonathan in the dominant. These roles were a natural progression due in part to our religious backgrounds, which clearly taught, "Wives, submit yourselves unto your own husbands, as it is fit in the Lord." (Colossians 3:19) Equally influential for me were the women I saw as role models, such as my mother, grandmother, and aunts. They were women, mostly housewives, who spent their lives being helpmates to their husbands.

Life with Jonathan centered around his goals: we moved so he could pursue his master's degree, then his Ph.D., then his career; we attended the church he chose; we lived according to the lifestyle he wanted; Jonathan controlled the household finances. Jonathan was the dominant one—head of our household. Yes, I always gave him my paycheck; all we had was considered jointly owned. (He even claimed the harpsichord that I had paid for with my piano student money). I attended his church, which after our fourth year of marriage was usually against my will. I was the submissive, dutiful wife who eventually grew out of my role and began to rebel. Had our marriage developed an equality, it would have been more healthy. However, I doubt this could have happened within the confines of Jonathan's religion, a religion I had gradually come to reject.

By the end of my marriage I felt that I had given all I could give to Jonathan and that there was no more left. I had supported Jonathan through nine years of school while working full time and performing the domestic duties of a housewife. This was in addition to participating excessively in Jonathan's church as a musician, choir director, and sometimes Sunday school teacher—without pay. By the end of Jonathan's Ph.D. program I could no longer force myself to fit into Jonathan's life. I had reached a crisis point. My nourishment had been depleted, and since Jonathan did not have the capacity to replenish what had been taken, I had to leave. Although it took me six years (including separation) to believe that I had made the right decision, there is no doubt now that leaving Jonathan was the best thing for me. He was a good person, but he was not right for me.

Leaving Jonathan and removing myself from his church's influence were the first two steps toward obtaining the proper equilibrium necessary for my own health. While being away from both influences, I have restructured my religious beliefs, become more sensitive to my needs, and, fortunately, I have been successful in meeting nearly all of them.

During the most painful part of my divorce, when I prayed to God for comfort and strength, I believed that the magnitude of pain I suffered was inversely proportional to the amount of joy I would experience in the future. That belief gave me hope during a time when my life was totally devastated. Whether it was my own strength and determination, luck, God's hand in my life, or a little of each that turned my situation around, these past few years have been the best in my life.

When I was married to Jonathan, I was an unassertive, half-person who had no control over her emotions or her life. I relied on external factors for reasoning and direction. But now my situation has changed, and I have changed. I have learned what I need for happiness, and I know how to achieve it. I have become a whole person, in control of my life! My time of great pain and suffering has turned into happiness; my faith was not in vain. The storm has ended, and as the sun's bright rays of warmth penetrate my life, I sing songs of thanksgiving, for my dreams have come true! "They that sow in tears shall reap in joy!" (Psalms 126:5)

Coda

During my year of research, when I read all my diaries from the beginning of my marriage through my divorce, I came upon an interesting discovery. Two years before I met Mario, I had a dream about an "unknown younger man." I noted it in my diary because during the dream I experienced a feeling of abundant love—love of which I felt very undeserving. After the dream I was puzzled, for there had been no younger man in my life who matched the person in my dream. Two years later, I met Mario, a younger man who blessed me with his gift of overwhelming love. Upon finding my diary entry, I realized the dream had been about him!

Another interesting discovery is that six months after my divorce I wrote the journal entry, "What is love? I have almost come to the conclusion that the love I seek does not exist." I had decided my longings were for a fantasy love that was unattainable. In my journal I had listed the following characteristics for my ideal companion: a mirror image of me in interests; one who adored me and satisfied my desire for romance and sex; one who was athletic, intelligent, sensitive, strong, and spoiling; musical and successful; mature but young. I had wanted someone with whom I could have an emotional connection, so that there would be intimacy. But I was disheartened because, "I know now that love is not the dream I once thought was reality." I had believed I was chasing a dream that could never come true. Yet as incredible as it may seem, seven years later, all the qualities I had listed for my ideal love were found in Mario! The love of which I had fantasized is now my reality. Literally, my dreams have come true. Is it any wonder that now "my cup runneth over" with great joy? (Psalms 23:5)

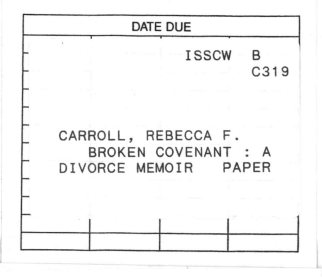